About Dorcas and This Book

WordPress Masterbook 2019
- Make a Website from Scratch for Total Beginners

by Dorcas Réamonn

Last Updated: 24th June 2019

Dorcas Réamonn is a lecturer in the UCD Michael Smurfit Graduate Business School (the graduate business school of University College Dublin Ireland), a trainer and consultant with Talentpool Ltd, and founder of Zonua. She has been teaching WordPress in classrooms for about seven years, and wrote her first WordPress book in 2017. As well as WordPress-related courses, Dorcas teaches in Image Editing, Video Creation, SEO and Digital Marketing. She has been making websites for about ten years.

This book is aimed at WordPress beginners, not professional website developers.

All themes and plugins recommended in this book are genuine recommendations, and the policy of this book is to recommend *only* free themes and plugins that are freely available on WordPress.org.

Suggestions on improvements to future editions of this book are genuinely most welcome.

To contact Dorcas quickly & directly, look for @zonua on Twitter. To check out some of the photos she's taken, look for @dorcasz on Instagram. Questions and requests are also dealt with on her YouTube Channel – www.youtube.com/zonua.

This book gets regularly updated (usually approximately once per month).

For all questions on WordPress, Dorcas invites all readers to join and interact in the WordPress support group:

» www.facebook.com/groups/WordPressMasterbook

Cover photo: by Dorcas Réamonn

All other pictures; Screen-captures taken from the WordPress dashboard for educational purposes.

For all the amazing students in MKT42200 and MKT42050, classes of 2019.

João Alves Reis, Laura Ashmore, Sophie Barron, Christopher Buckley, Jessica Burford, Sarah Burmanje, Seán Byrne, Cathyrn Caldwell, Michael Calvey, Irina Chakina, Sarah Collard, Kevin Curley, Aastha Gambhir, Muhammad Ghazi, Corinna Gross, Andrea Hall, Kuan-Hsin Hsiao, Yanqiao Ji, Leah Kelly, Harshit Khaitan, Jun Wei Kwen, Minh Dung Le, Sanna Larke, Wei Luo, Michelle McGuire, Sam Molony, Holly Newport, Hoang Minh Nguyen, Thi Nhat Anh Nguyen, Ciara O'Loughlin, Seamus O'Shea, Supriya Pillai, Pravitha Premraja, Zoe Rice, Michelle Roche, Anna Roopraninesingh, Elien Saelens, Zach Salveta, Emily Schaefer, Shikha Singh, Abhilasha Thorat, Catherina Viani

Aoife Bolger, Jack Dempsey, Vanisha Finlay, Ross Fitzpatrick, Emily Flanagan, Michelle Frahill, Anurag Goyal, Fabienne Jackson, Yixuan Ji, Clodagh Kenny, Gillian Kiely, Ellen Kilgallon, Alex Kirker, Abigail Kuyebi, Kerrie Leonard, Seamus McDermott, Holly McQuillan, Rebecca Millar, Andrew Murphy, Niamh O'Connor, Alison O'Gorman, Dianaimh Phelan, Simon Phillips, Grace Power, Robyn Reddy, Jennifer Roberts, Doruk Tort, Jamie Thomas, Caroline Walsh

"Any useful idea about the future should appear to be ridiculous"

– Jim Dator, Futurist

A Note from the Author

Hi!
I'm Dorcas.

Once upon a time, I didn't know much about making websites, just like
you. There was even a time when I knew nothing about making websites
– hell, there was even a time when I hadn't even heard of WordPress!
The point I want to make is, if I can learn, so can you.

I've written this book for the non-technical total beginner. I'm assuming
you already know how to use the internet, surf the web, type, use search
engines like Google - but I'm assuming you know nothing about making
websites.

I'm not claiming this is the best WordPress book in the world (maybe it
is, I dunno), but some people like my style of teaching.

I gather the questions that I get both in real life and online, from my face-
to-face classes and consultations, and compile information from my own
day-to-day work with WordPress. This has resulted in a serious,
comprehensive, but easy-to-follow WordPress book.

To contact me quickly, look for @zonua on Twitter. Suggestions on
improvements to future editions of this book are genuinely welcome.

For all questions on WordPress, please join and partake in the group:

www.facebook.com/groups/WordPressMasterbook

I'd be delighted if you posted the link of your new website in that group!

Please also check out the final section in this book, Additional
Resources, for access to a free e-learning course I'm developing, that is
based on this book!

Finally, if you don't like this book, or think there's anything I can improve upon (whether it's a tiny thing or a big thing), please, please let me know. Really. It's only with negative feedback that I can improve. If you give me any sort of feedback that helps me improve, I'll get you a free copy of my next book, and a big thanks! You can email me directly at **books@golearndigital.com**.

Enjoy the book,

Oscar

There are three things you need, if you wish to proceed.

1. You should be a little **nerdy**; that is, you need to enjoy learning, enjoy working at a desk, enjoy solving problems, enjoy working on a computer. I'm a big nerd so I love all this kind of stuff.

2. You need to be **interested,** you need to like it. If you don't enjoy making the website, quit, and spend your time doing things you actually enjoy. Just as, when it comes to fixing your car or painting your house – you either pay someone or do it yourself. Don't beat yourself if you're not they type of person who wants to make websites.

3. **Go easy on yourself**! It's okay to be frustrated! It's okay not to be able to find that button immediately! If you find yourself getting frustrated, walk away and come back later.

Contents

13

How to Use this Book

This book is aimed at beginners, who are making a WordPress website for the first time. This book covers the basics you need to know to get started. The chapters are laid out roughly in the correct order, however feel free to skip over the parts that are not relevant to you.

Following Along

Sometimes we have included screen captures from WordPress.

When instructions are in text to click on links, they are in the format like this.

E.g. To Change your Menu settings, go to: *Appearance > Menus*

… which means you should click first on Appearance, and then secondly on Menus. The first word will always be in the main menu of your Dashboard.

Some Lingo:

WordPress: This book **always** refers to the CMS WordPress, and **not** the website builder on WordPress.com. Resources are at WordPress.org.

Dashboard: The Admin Panel. This is what you see when you login to your WordPress website as the administrator.

Chapter 1: What is WordPress?

WordPress is a CMS.

CMS stands for Content Management System.

There are different ways to make websites these days;

1. Learn code (e.g. HTML, CSS, PHP, Javascript, AJAX)
2. Use a Content Management System (CMS)
3. Use a Website Builder

First of all, I must explain the difference between a CMS and a Website Builder.

A website builder is a website where they take care of the hosting, and you build your website online via the website.

Some website builder websites include;

Often, you might buy your own domain and hosting for email locally, but attach the website-builder website to your domain, meaning that it will still be hosted with the website builder like Squarespace/Wix etc.

Some Content Management Systems are;

With a content management system, you need to have your own domain and your own hosting. The CMS is then installed onto your website. This gives you more control.

All of these Content Management Systems are great. This book is about one CMS, WordPress.

If you are serious about what you are doing, you should consider a CMS.

While website builders are often easier to use, they are often more restrictive, and you surrender a lot of control.

WordPress is the most popular CMS in the world, and it's open-source, which means it's free – good reasons to choose WordPress!

Important: When you install WordPress, you are using the WordPress at **WordPress.org, not** WordPress.com. It's very important that you know this, because when you search online for further, specific help, you need to know that any mention of WordPress.com is **not** relevant for you.

Chapter 2: Setting Up

Warning, this part is usually the most frustrating part for people, and you wouldn't be forgiven for asking a website developer or similar nerd to organise this for you.

Every WordPress website needs a domain and hosting. In theory you can actually set up your own computer to act as the host, but unless you've done this before, I wouldn't recommend you try. So, you need your domain and hosting, so that you can install WordPress.

The one piece of advice I would give, is, and you do this at the time of installation – change the default login from admin to *anything else*. 'Admin' is the default login for every WordPress in the world. So, if you were a hacker, you could try a brute-force attack to login with the username 'Admin'. That's why changing the username to anything else is a good idea.

By the way, the username, just like the password, is case-sensitive.

If your domain is www.example.com, but you don't want people to see your website there until you are ready, you can install WordPress onto a folder, like www.example.com/new, and work there until you are ready.

Hosting

When picking your hosting company, check out their support. Also, find out where their servers are – you should host your website as close as possible to your potential customers. If you are not sure where your website is hosted, you can check with

» www.infosniper.net.

I'm based in Ireland, I have experience with a lot of companies, my favourite is Blacknight, they are brilliant in terms of support.

What Type of Hosting Do I Need?
You need hosting with PHP support. Specifically, ideally PHP version

7.0, but at least PHP version 5.6.

You need a database. Every WordPress website needs a database.

If you have a choice between Windows or Linux servers – go with Linux. This is irrelevant to the type of laptop/device that you have.

Most hosting companies these days have an easy one-click installation.

For information on manual installation, check out https://codex.WordPress.org/Installing_WordPress

Special Offer
Letshost area a great hosting company with servers in Ireland. Their customer service is excellent. I asked them for a discount code – and they gave it to me. DM me on Twitter (@zonua) and I'll let you know the latest discount for 50% off their WordPress package.

Note: As with everything in this book, this is not affiliate marketing, I get no rewards for sharing this discount code with you.

SSL Certificate
You may also need to think about an SSL certificate: this means your website will be secure, and will be accessed via https:// instead of http://.

When I say may – if you are thinking of getting e-commerce – definitely get an SSL certificate. For brochure-style websites, SSL certificates are soon becoming a necessity rather than an option – you'll rank better in Google with an SSL certificate, and I've seen Chrome warn users that the website is 'Not Secure' when the website is not on https – that could turn visitors away from your website.

Websites on an SSL certificate will have the little lock icon appear in the browser, to show visitors that it is secure;

So, to summarise, if you have an e-commerce website, or are handling sensitive/personal data via the website, then you definitely need an SSL certificate. Google likes secure certificates, so having a secure website will help you rank better.

Where to get an SSL Certificate
The easiest place to get your SSL certificate is from the same place as your host – i.e. buy from the company hosting your website. You need to pay for your SSL certificate every year, generally the price range is something like;

- €30 - €100 per year
- £25 - £100 per year
- USD$30 – USD$100 per year

What happens if I don't renew my SSL Certificate?
if it expires, your website visitors could see a scary looking page like this:

Your connection is not private

Attackers might be trying to steal your information from **www.** ███████ (for example, passwords, messages, or credit cards). <u>Learn more</u>

NET::ERR_CERT_DATE_INVALID

☐ Help improve Safe Browsing by sending some <u>system information and page content</u> to Google. <u>Privacy policy</u>

ADVANCED   Back to safety

And something like this would appear up in the address bar:

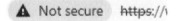

So … it's important to remember to new your SSL certificate every year (or just set up an auto-renew).

Emails

This section is not strictly related to WordPress, but this topic is often asked when people are setting up their first WordPress host.

Once you have a domain name and hosting you can get emails like info@example.com or joe@example.com – anything you like.

Each hosting company has different systems. For example, with Blacknight, check your emails from any computer at »
altmail.blacknight.com

Set up a new email address by logging into your host (e.g. for Blacknight login to cp.blacknight.com and then go to Email > Add New E-mail Address).

To set up email onto your phone/Outlook/tablet etc. you need details similar to this:

POP server: pop33.cp.blacknight.com
IMAP server: imap5r.cp.blacknight.com
SMTP server: smtp1r.cp.blacknight.com

POP and IMAP are for incoming mails, SMTP is for the outgoing mails.

Note: I recommend IMAP over POP.

The username is usually your email address, the password is as you set it. You need to set the username and password for both incoming and outgoing mails, even if they are the same (in most cases, they are). Double-check to verify that you can send and receive emails.

If you are using hosting with another company, then you need to ask them for their details – ask for the incoming server and outgoing server details for your mails.

What ports to use
When setting up your email with If you are on a secure server, then you may need to ask your hosting company which ports to use. Sometimes the default in Outlook/your phone will work, and you don't need to worry about changing the ports. However, if emails are not being sent/received, and you are sure you put in the correct username, server and password, then you should probably check the ports.

IMAP ports:

- 143
- 993 (SSL)

POP ports:

- 110
- 995 (SSL)

SMTP ports:

- 587 (usually a better option than 25)
- 25 (some network providers block outgoing mails from port 25, as a measure to cut down on spam)
- 465 (SSL)

Installing WordPress

There are two ways to install WordPress.

The first way is manually: See the WordPress codex for instructions:

» https://codex.WordPress.org/Installing_WordPress

Personally, I install all of my WordPress websites manually. It gives me a little more control.

The second, but actually most common way, is automatically.

Most good hosting companies have an easy-install, so you don't actually need to manually install yourself. Look for something like 'one-click install'.

Contact your host to find out how to do this. It's very easy and will take you a few minutes; for Example, with Blacknight CPanel, go to: Applications > WordPress > Install: Choose Your Domain, click next: Leave the 'URL path' blank to install straight onto your domain.

Because the automated install will be different for each host, this book does not cover installation. Automated installation is a five-minute job for someone who knows the relevant system, so your host might not even charge for installation.

If you are stuck – ask us in our Facebook support group (see Additional Resources for the link).

Chapter 3: Introduction to the Dashboard

The dashboard is what you see when you log in to the Administrator side of your website. The visitor to your website won't see the dashboard. You need to access the dashboard to make any changes to your website.

Accessing the Dashboard

Once you have WordPress installed on your domain, then you can login to the website panel at www.yourwebsite.com/**wp-admin**, where www.yourwebsite.com is the folder where you installed WordPress. So, if you installed WordPress at a folder called 'new', then you should go to www.yourwebsite.com/new/wp-admin.

Dashboard Overview

The dashboard is what you see when you login to your website, and will look like this;

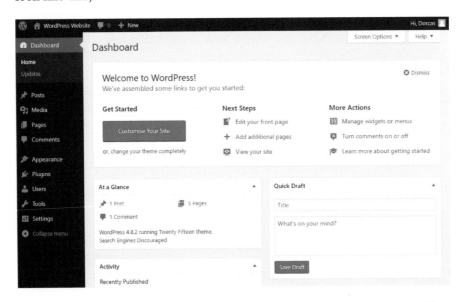

On the left-hand side, you will see the navigation menu, like this;

Sometimes, I've noticed beginners 'lose' this menu, and the left-hand side of their Dashboard screen will look like this;

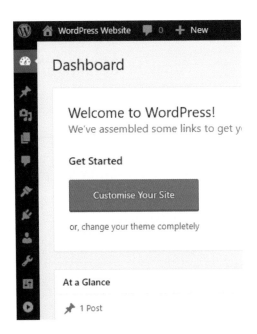

Simply click the icon at the bottom, to expand the menu, so that you can see the standard menu with text:

The biggest tip I could give to a beginner at this stage, is to have two Windows, or two tabs open; one with the Dashboard, and one with the live website, so you can see the changes as you work.

Sometimes, some people ask me how to get rid of the black bar at the top with the login details at the top of the website, like this:

You don't need to. That's only visible for you, when you are logged in to your website. Other people won't see that black bar on your website.

Chapter 4: Setting Up for the First Time

Set the Site Title

Go to: *Settings > General*: Change the Site Title and Tagline

Site Title	WordPress Website

Tagline	Just another WordPress site
	In a few words, explain what this site is about.

Click **Save Changes** at the bottom of the page.

Danger!

See the fields here?

WordPress Address (URL)	http://zonua.ie/test
Site Address (URL)	http://zonua.ie/test

You'll find them in *Settings > General*. Don't change them unless you know what you're doing. In other words, don't change them. Even changing a character could make your whole website go blank, you lose the dashboard ... your website disappears ... it's not nice. Yes, you can get it back, but then you need to do techy things like accessing the database ... it's easier if you just never ever change these fields.

Nice URLs

Ensure you can get nice URLs in your page links, other than the default.

> The default in WordPress is that the link of the page will be something like yourwebsite.com/pageid=12 -
>
> It's better to set the default so that the link of the page will automatically include the word in the heading. To do this, go to
>
> Go to: *Settings > Permalinks*: Click Post name so that **/%postname%/** appears in 'Custom Structure' like this;

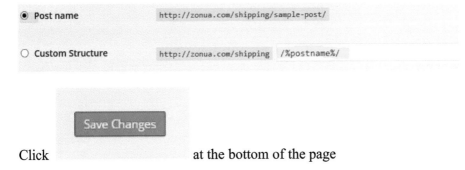

Click ⬚⬚⬚⬚⬚⬚ at the bottom of the page

Creating the Homepage

The homepage is the page that visitors arrive on when they go directly to www.yourwebsite.com.

Note: Some people call the homepage a 'landing page', however I prefer not to use that term, as it's not necessarily correct. The landing page refers to the page that you land upon, when you visit a website. So, if you type www.website.com in your browser, then sure, you land on the homepage. But, oftentimes, via a search in Google, you don't arrive on the homepage; for example, you could arrive on a product page – in that case, that's the landing page. So – the homepage is only the landing page if that's the page a visitor initially sees. In other contexts, a landing page could be a totally different page.

And, to make things more complicated, when you're talking in the context of digital marketing, generally a landing page is a standalone web page which is created specifically for an advertising or marketing campaign, for example if you were running Google Ads, a Facebook competition, or special offer.

Generally speaking, the homepage on your website is going to be much fancier than the other pages, and you will spend much more time on the homepage than any other page.

There are two parts to creating the homepage in WordPress; first, you have to create the page, then you have to actually tell the 'system' that this is the homepage.

- So, as in the start of this chapter, create page, call it Home (or whatever you want), and save it by clicking 'Publish';

  You can worry about the actual content of the page later – for now, you are just creating a page, and assigning it to the homepage.
- Next, go to: *Appearance > Customise:*
- Scroll down until you see 'Static Front Page'. Select 'A static page' instead of 'Your latest posts', and then select the page that just saved to be the homepage.

Homepage Settings   >

Choose 'A static page' instead of 'Your latest posts', and then, in the dropdown, choose the page you just made, like this;

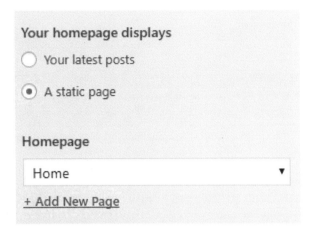

This page will now be visible on the homepage of your website.

Chapter 5: Themes

A theme in WordPress means 'template'.

The template determines the layout and appearance of the website.

Only ever get a *free* theme from WordPress.org.

If you want to *buy* a theme, I mostly use www.themeforest.net.

If you change a theme on your website, the appearance will change, but the content will remain the same.

The default theme that will be preinstalled from 6th December 2019 is 'Twenty Nineteen' – but nobody uses the default theme. (Okay, I'm sure you can prove me wrong if you really want to, but I've never heard of or seen a 'real live website' use any of the default WordPress themes.)

Tips Picking a Theme on WordPress.org/themes

1. Popularity: Look at 'Active Installs' (or Purchases for a paid-for themes)
   Pick a popular theme, it is less likely to have glitches, and more likely that you will find support. Generally, I wouldn't recommend a beginner pick a theme with less than 5,000 downloads.

2. Ratings: Look at the star-rating as well as number of votes

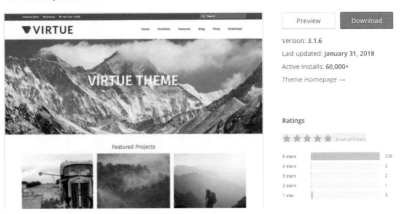

3. Description: Make sure it's responsive.
   Note: I'm not sure I even need to say this anymore, you'd be hard-pushed to find a theme in 2019 that isn't responsive.

Virtue *By Kadence Themes*

The Virtue theme is extremely versatile with tons of options, easy to customize and loaded with great features. Virtue has Schema microdata integrated making it a step ahead for your sites SEO ranks. The clean modern design is built with html5 and css3 and uses the powerful responsive framework from Bootstrap to be a fully responsive and mobile friendly. It's fully ecommerce (Woocommerce) ready with all the tools you need to design an awesome online store. The versatile design is perfect for any kind of business, online store, portfolio or personal site. Virtue is Schema ready. We built Virtue with a powerful options panel where you can set things like your home layout, sliders, custom fonts, and completely customize your look without writing any CSS. You are going to love how easy this theme is to work with. Virtue was built and designed by Kadence Themes.

4. Demo: A lot of the time, the Preview on www.WordPress.org is pretty useless, you need to click on 'Themes Homepage' and hope that the makers of the theme have a decent demo.

Virtue *By Kadence Themes*

5. Google is your friend: Search for theme recommendations and read reviews on third-party websites.
6. See Recommended Free Themes for my recommendations.

Installing a Theme.

When you have chosen the theme you want to use, it needs to be installed, and activated.

I recommend you only ever get a free theme from WordPress.org. These themes have been through a control process. If you get a free theme from elsewhere, you are leaving your website more vulnerable.

Using a Paid-for Theme
If you have bought a theme, you will be provided a ZIP file. Don't unzip this file.

1. Go to: *Appearance > Themes > Add New > Upload Theme*

2. Upload the ZIP file of the theme
3. Activate the theme once installed.

Using a Free Theme
To install any of the free WordPress themes in the following section, *you don't need to download from WordPress.org*:

To use one of these themes;

1. Go to*: Appearance > Themes* in your Dashboard.
2. Click 'Add New'
3. Then, in the search box, you will be able to find all of the themes found on WordPress.org: simply type the name of the theme you want.

4. Hover over the Install the theme you want, and click 'Install'.
5. Once Installed, Activate the theme

Recommended Free Themes

All of these themes in the following section are available from WordPress.org/themes. This means, that to install them, you simply need to start at *Appearances > Themes > Add New.*

Note, these are listed in a random order.

Note: If you think that you are not ready to add an e-commerce side to your website, but want to some time I in the future, it will make your life much easier if you pick a theme that is e-commerce, or, more specifically, WooCommerce ready.

Standard Brochure;
- Virtue » https://wordpress.org/themes/virtue
- Spacious » https://wordpress.org/themes/spacious
- Ample by ThemeGrill » https://wordpress.org/themes/ample
- Pinnacle » https://wordpress.org/themes/pinnacle
- Vantage » https://wordpress.org/themes/vantage
- Radiate » https://wordpress.org/themes/radiate
- Attitude » https://wordpress.org/themes/attitude
- Auberge » https://wordpress.org/themes/auberge
- Customizr » https://wordpress.org/themes/customizr
- Sydney » https://wordpress.org/themes/sydney
- GeneratePress » https://wordpress.org/themes/generatepress
- Hestia » https://wordpress.com/themes/hestia

E-Commerce (some of the previous themes are also ready for E-Commerce)

- eStore » https://wordpress.org/themes/estore
- Storefront » https://wordpress.org/themes/storefront
- MaxStore » https://wordpress.org/themes/maxstore
- Hestia » https://wordpress.com/themes/hestia
- Virtue » https://wordpress.org/themes/virtue

Magazine;

- Colormag » https://wordpress.org/themes/colormag
- Newsmag » https://wordpress.org/themes/newsmag

Blogging;

- Olsen Light » https://wordpress.org/themes/olsen-light
- Garfunkel » https://wordpress.org/themes/hueman
- Fashionistas » https://wordpress.org/themes/fashionistas
- Garfunkel » https://wordpress.org/themes/garfunkel

Portfolio;

- Pictorio » https://wordpress.org/themes/pictorico
- GK Portfolio » https://wordpress.org/themes/gk-portfolio
- Portfolio Press » https://wordpress.org/themes/portfolio-press

One-Pagers;

- Zerif-Lite by Themeisle - » https://wordpress.org/themes/zerif-lite

- OnePress by FameThemes - » https://wordpress.org/themes/onepress
- Onetone by MageeWP - » https://wordpress.org/themes/onetone
- Vega by lyrathemes - » https://wordpress.org/themes/vega
- Hestia » https://wordpress.com/themes/hestia

Particularly Versatile Themes

Virtue

Support forum: » **https://wordpress.org/support/theme/virtue**

Author's website: » **http://www.kadencethemes.com/product/virtue-free-theme/**

Vantage

Support forum: » **https://wordpress.org/support/theme/vantage**

Author's website: » **https://siteorigin.com/theme/vantage/**

How to Check What Theme You are Using

It's important to know what theme you are using. The theme determines the layout of your site. To change the appearance of your site, you need to go into the settings of the theme.

To find out what theme you are using, go to: *Appearance > Themes*

The first theme that appears is the one that your site is using;

From the picture above, I can see the theme that I'm using here is 'Twenty Nineteen'. I can also tell this theme is the one my theme is using because it says 'Active'.

Active means that is the current theme my website using.

Chapter 6: Pages

Pages

For static pages on your website, you want use **Pages**. Static pages are the pages like the 'About' or 'Contact' pages.

Note: If you are only interested in blogging, go to Chapter 5: Blogging

Note: For e-commerce, go to Chapter 15: E-Commerce.

To add a new page, go to: *Pages > Add New:*

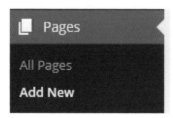

Now, we're at the first part in this book where you need to make a decision for yourself in terms of how you're going to proceed. You need to decide which 'Page Builder' you're going to use. First, you need to understand what a Page Builder actually is – continue to the next chapter.

Chapter 7: Page Builders & Editors

Right, before we talk specifically, let's talk generally. What's this chapter about anyway?

You create a page – and you want to decide what appears on the page:

However, let's say you wanted something fancier like this, like a certain place on your page that has a purple background, and a picture that appears on the left-hand side.

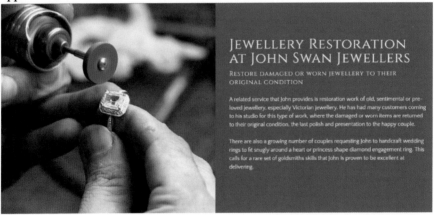

Screen-capture of page from diamondjewellers.ie on desktop. Used with permission

And then you realise that this won't really work on mobiles, so you decide you want something like this, with the image first and the text afterwards for mobiles … (see next page) …

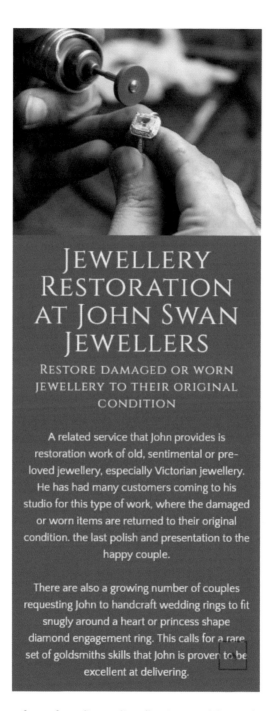

JEWELLERY RESTORATION AT JOHN SWAN JEWELLERS

RESTORE DAMAGED OR WORN JEWELLERY TO THEIR ORIGINAL CONDITION

A related service that John provides is restoration work of old, sentimental or pre-loved jewellery, especially Victorian jewellery. He has had many customers coming to his studio for this type of work, where the damaged or worn items are returned to their original condition. the last polish and presentation to the happy couple.

There are also a growing number of couples requesting John to handcraft wedding rings to fit snugly around a heart or princess shape diamond engagement ring. This calls for a rare set of goldsmiths skills that John is proven to be excellent at delivering.

Screen-capture of page from diamondjewellers.ie on mobile. Used with permission

… you need a fancier editor than the 'Classic Editor'. You need either Gutenberg or another Page Builder.

This decision divides people. If you're new to WordPress, you may not mind Gutenberg so much. If you're already familiar with the previous editor, you may hate Gutenberg.

In 2018 I deliberately didn't cover Gutenberg in my WordPress book or teachings. I didn't like Gutenberg, and I wasn't the only one: It was getting bad feedback, bad reviews, it's buggy, and it's not as good as the other page-builders out there. The current rating (January 2019) is about 2 out of 5 at the moment – which is pretty bad …

Gutenberg

 (1,441)

A new editing experience for WordPress is in the works, with the goal of making it easier than ever to make your words, pictures, and layout look just …

Gutenberg Team

500,000+ active installations   Tested with 4.9.8

Screen capture from http://wordpress.org/plugins/gutenberg from November 2018

Without labouring the point … a search in the plugins on WordPress.org shows these two plugins as the top results;

Gutenberg
★★☆☆☆ (2,350)
A new editing experience for WordPress is in the works, with the goal of making it easier than ever to make your words, pictures, and layout look just …

Gutenberg Team
200,000+ active installations   Tested with 5.0.3

Disable Gutenberg
★★★★★ (292)
Disable Gutenberg Block Editor and restore the Classic Editor and original Edit Post screen (TinyMCE, meta boxes, et al). Selectively disable for post …

Jeff Starr
100,000+ active installations   Tested with 5.0.3

Screen captures from http://wordpress.org/plugins/gutenberg from November 2018

What is Gutenberg?

- It's the new Editor for WordPress. The Editor is where you normally write the content for your page. Gutenberg would replace current editor, which is now being referred to as 'Classic Editor'.

- It's part of WordPress since WordPress 5.0, which was launched in December 2018.

Gutenberg FAQs

Q. Why would someone disable Gutenberg?

A. There could be backward-compatibility issues, particularly with plugins you are currently using.

A. Some people just don't like it and prefer to use other options.

Q. Where can I get more information?

A. https://wordpress.org/gutenberg/ is the official resource.

Q. When will Gutenberg be released?

Since December 2018, it's part of actual WordPress – meaning, when you begin using WordPress you'll see the Gutenberg editor and not the usual one.

If you join our Facebook support group at **www.facebook.com/groups/WordPressMasterbook**- then we'll be sure to post updates there.

Gutenberg

How to use Gutenberg

The Gutenberg editor looks like this:

This section is where you add the content of your page:

Click on a section to edit it.

That's all I'm covering. As you may have guessed from the previous section, I don't use Gutenberg and I don't like it. I don't see the benefit to teaching you how to use it – there are other better options.

Classic Editor

How to Activate Classic Editor

If you're using WordPress 5.0 or higher then you'll automatically be on Gutenberg (unless you've changed it. Before we cover how to use the Classic Editor, you can disable Gutenberg to use the Classic Editor by installing a plugin.

Go to *Plugins > Add New*. Search for 'Classic Editor' and make sure you find the one called Classic Editor by WordPress Contributors. Install and activate this plugin to use the 'old' WordPress Editor instead of Gutenberg. You'll see by the popularity of this plugin that there are many people who simply don't like Gutenberg!

How to Use Classic Editor

This field is the h1 heading on your webpage.

Add New Page

Enter title here

The h1 heading is the Heading 1 in HTML. Try to choose a descriptive heading here, that includes your search terms.

Therefore, think about getting your search terms in there.

In the section below, we have the 'content' of our page:

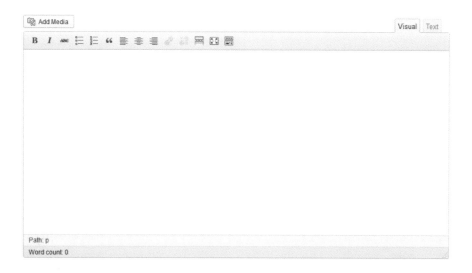

We have no excuse for not getting our search terms into that section.

Saving a Page

To save a page, click 'Publish'. Note that sometimes this button may say 'Update'. These are just WordPress words for 'save'.

Viewing the page

There are two ways to view the page on your website. One is the quick way, and one is the longer way, but it's better.

To view the page, on the right-hand side, close to where you clicked 'Publish', you can click 'Preview Changes'.

This will open a new tab, where you can view the changes that you have done.

However, the *better way* to view a page, is to first create a Menu, and add it to the Menu.

When I'm teaching my WordPress class, I recommend my students to quickly just create pages by putting in the h1 heading and some dummy text in the content, saving the page – and then creating the menu, and then they can come back and edit the content of the page.

To see how to create a Menu: Chapter 6: Menus

Page Links

The permalink of the page is the link of that individual page.

Get your search terms into that link, by 'editing' the link.

Permalink: http://talentpoolltd.ie/blog/contact-us/ [Edit]

If your page is already doing okay/well in search engine results, then do not change this link. You want to pick your link in the beginning, and do not change it in the future.

If the link of the page will be something like yourwebsite.com/pageid=12, then you need to change the permalink settings (see here: Chapter 4: Nice URLs).

Add a picture

To add a picture to the content, put the cursor in the text box where you want the image to go:

My picture goes under this paragraph

|

And over this paragraph.

Click 'Add Media':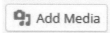

Choose between 'Upload Files' or 'Media Library';

Insert Media

Upload Files | Media Library

The Media Library contains files that have already been uploaded to your site. Choose 'Upload Files' to upload a picture to your website for the first time.

Once you have uploaded/selected a picture, click 'Insert into page', at the bottom right hand corner of your screen.  or

Insert into page

To edit the Caption, Alternative Text, and Title for that image, click on the image. You will then see an 'edit' and a 'remove' button, which will look like this

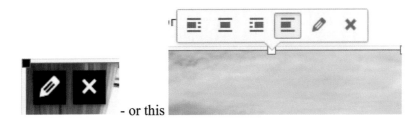

 - or this

Choose the 'edit' button that is shaped like a pencil

If you want a caption, fill in the caption field:

The 'alt', or 'alternate text' goes in this field:

The title, which is what people see if they hover over the image, goes here (note that you may need to click 'Advanced Options' to see this field.

Remember that the Alternative and Title are important for SEO.

Click update when you are finished editing. You can come back and change these at any time.

Adding a link within a page
Where appropriate – link.

- for more information, contact us!

If that was the text on our website, it would make sense to link that text to the contact page. To do so, select the text, and then click this icon:

Then, click on the little cog icon that appears:

To link to a page within your website: Under 'Or link to existing content', find the page you want to link to; select it by clicking once, and then click 'Add Link';

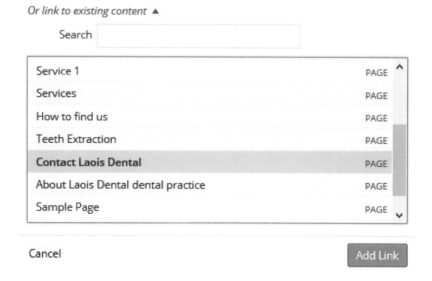

To link to an external page (i.e. a page that is not on your website, e.g. www.facebook.com/yourbusinesspage) - then you have to make sure you include the http:// beforehand. Otherwise the link won't work.

When linking to external pages on your website, select 'Open link in a new tab';

Enter the destination URL

Always check your links. If your external links give a 'page not found', check the link, and make sure you have put in http:// before the www.

Page Layout

The theme determines the layout, however the typical layout is that every page (apart from the homepage) will have a sidebar – typically on the right hand side of the page. To change the content of the sidebar, go to *Appearance > Widgets*.

to actually remove the whole sidebar from your page, go to the page, and on the right hand side, look for the section called 'Page Attributes'.

In the section 'Page Attributes', you will see 'Template', and in the dropdown underneath 'Template', change from 'Default Template'.

Depending on your theme, you may have different page types, for example, in Virtue you can choose 'Fullwidth', or in Vantage, you can choose 'Full Width Page' – if you are not sure how the new layout will look – save it and view it.

Page Builder by Site Origin

I'm not going to go a 'how to use the Page Builder' – that's another book in itself, but SiteOrigin themselves have loads and loads of resources including videos and tutorials, that you can check out here: https://siteorigin.com/page-builder/

So, here, I'm just pointing out two things that aren't covered (as far as I can see!) in the SiteOrigin information, and they're two things that you aren't obvious.

Switching between Page Builder and the 'Other Editor':
A nice feature with Page Builder by Site Origin is that, for any page, you can revert to the 'Classic Editor' (the editor that was inbuilt into WordPress in the pre-Gutenberg days), with this plugin, by clicking on 'Revert to Editor':

Now you'll see the 'traditional classic editor'. If you want to use the Page Builder, then you can click 'Page Builder';

This means that you can use the Page Builder on your 'fancier' pages, but still use the classic editor for pages that only require a more simple layout.

Top tip!

I just learned this today (February 2019) – right-click and you can add rows and widgets easily, like this:

Chapter 8: Blogging

Posts

Posts are quite similar to pages, but are specifically for blog articles. Hence, you don't want to use 'Posts' unless you are going to have a blog section on your website.

So ... of course ... if you plan on blogging, then you will use this Posts section, if you don't plan on blogging, then you can ignore Posts.

The good news is that WordPress was originally made for blog websites. However WordPress eventually became so good and versatile, that people started using it for real, brochure and e-commerce websites.

In WordPress, each blog article is called Post.

To add your first Post, go to: *Posts > Add New:*

Make sure that you're clicking on 'Posts', and not 'Pages' – as the layout looks almost identical.

Just like with Pages, this field is the h1 heading on your webpage.

Add a New Post

Enter title here

When people share your blog post across their social media profiles, like Facebook or Twitter, this is the text that will automatically appear.

Therefore, think about getting your search terms in there.

In the section below, we have the 'content' of our page:

We have no excuse for not getting our search terms into that section.

Saving a Page

To save a page, click 'Publish'. Note that sometimes this button may say 'Update'. These are just WordPress words for 'save'.

Page Links

The permalink of the page is the link of that individual page.

Get your search terms into that link, by 'editing' the link.

If your page is already doing okay/well in search engine results, then do not change this link. You want to pick your link in the beginning, and do not change it in the future.

If the link of the page will be something like yourwebsite.com/pageid=12, then you need to change the permalink settings: Ensure you can get nice URLs in your page links, other than the default.

Add a picture

To add a picture to the content, put the cursor in the text box where you want the image to go:

My picture goes under this paragraph

|

And over this paragraph.

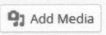

Click 'Add Media':

Choose between 'Upload Files' or 'Media Library';

Insert Media

Upload Files   Media Library

The Media Library contains files that have already been uploaded to your site. Choose 'Upload Files' to upload a picture to your website for the first time.

Once you have uploaded/selected a picture, click 'Insert into page', at the bottom right hand corner of your screen. **Insert into post** or

Insert into page

To edit the Caption, Alternative Text, and Title for that image, click on the image. You will then see an 'edit' and a 'remove' button, which will look like this

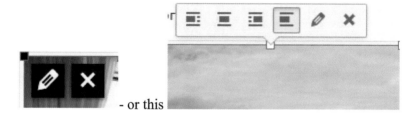

 - or this

Choose the 'edit' button that is shaped like a pencil

If you want a caption, fill in the caption field:

Caption | |

The 'alt', or 'alternate text' goes in this field:

Alternative Text

The title, which is what people see if they hover over the image, goes here (note that you may need to click 'Advanced Options' to see this field.

Image Title Attribute

Remember that the Alternative and Title are important for SEO.

Click update when you are finished editing. You can come back and change these at any time.

Update

Adding a link within a page
Where appropriate – link.

- for more information, contact us!

If that was the text on our website, it would make sense to link that text to the contact page. To do so, select the text, and then click this icon:

Then, click on the little cog icon that appears:

To link to a page within your website: Under 'Or link to existing content', find the page you want to link to; select it by clicking once, and then click 'Add Link';

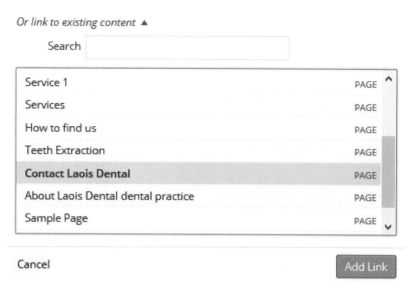

To link to an external page (i.e. a page that is not on your website, e.g. www.facebook.com/yourbusinesspage) - then you have to make sure you include the http:// beforehand. Otherwise the link won't work.

When linking to external pages on your website, select 'Open link in a new tab';

Always check your links. If your external links give a 'page not found', check the link, and make sure you have put in http:// before the www.

Page Layout

The theme determines the layout, however the typical layout is that every page (apart from the homepage) will have a sidebar – typically on the right hand side of the page. To change the content of the sidebar, go to *Appearance > Widgets.*

to actually remove the whole sidebar from your page, go to the page, and on the right-hand side, look for the section called 'Page Attributes'.

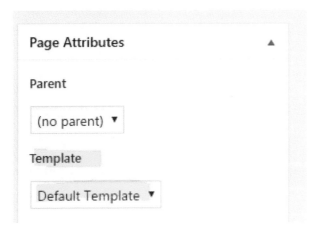

In the section 'Page Attributes', you will see 'Template', and in the dropdown underneath 'Template', change from 'Default Template'. Depending on your theme, you may have different page types, for example, in Virtue you can choose 'Fullwidth', or in Vantage, you can choose 'Full Width Page' – if you are not sure how the new layout will look – save it and view it.

Categories

Use categories so that eventually people can click to read all *blogs* about a certain topic. You probably don't need categories unless you are using the **Posts** part of your WordPress site.

Create a Category

To create a new category, go to: *Posts > Categories*

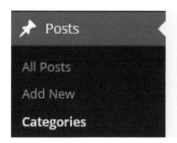

Fill in the fields 'Add new Category' (which is the name of the category), and 'slug' (which is the link the category page will have).

The 'Slug' is the link of the page. This is where you can get your SEO terms in. E.g. if you want the Category Name to be 'Blog' (this might be what you would rename 'All Categories' as) then you can call the slug seo-terms-blog – where of course 'seo-terms' are your own search terms.

In the slug

- Use lowercase

- No spaces
- Use dashes – or underscores _ between words, like this; directions-to-ireland

Leave 'Parent' as 'None' unless it is a sub-category:

Click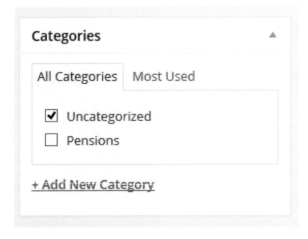

Don't worry too much about getting categories right at the start. You can add new ones at any time, delete ones you don't like. You can retrospectively add an old blog to a new category.

Add a Post to a Category

To add a post to a category, go to to the individual post, and look for this section, towards the right hand side of the screen …

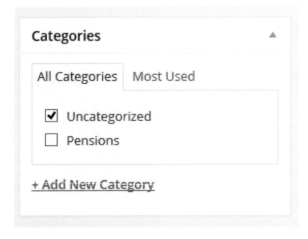

… and select the relevant category/categories:

To Add Multiple Posts to a Category/Categories

If you have created a new category after the posts are already created, you can add multiple posts to the same category.

First, create the category (Create a Category)

Secondly, go to: *Posts* > *All Posts*

Select the posts that you want to move to the category, by checking the

box before the post;

Next, where it says 'Bulk Actions', choose 'Edit from the dropdown menu;

Click 'Apply'

A new section will appear at the top of the page, like this;

In the Categories section, select the relevant category, and click the 'Update' button:

Chapter 9: Menus

To edit the menu in WordPress, go to: *Appearance > Menus*

Note: You need to create the pages before you add them to the menu.

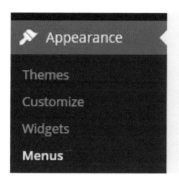

Note: Your Theme may already have a 'default menu'. You will definitely need to edit this, since the default setting is that this menu adds the pages in the order that you created them, without any proper structure.

Depending on your theme, you might have to add or edit the existing menu. If you do some changes here, and then don't see them on the website preview, then scroll to the bottom of the page, and look for something like 'Primary Menu' or 'Header Menu' and ensure that is ticked;

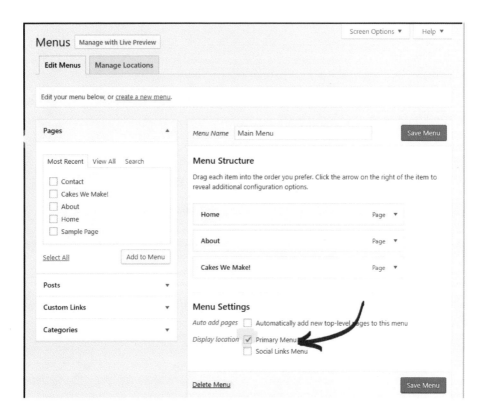

Different themes have different locations, so you could also see more options, something like this;

Menu Settings

Auto add pages ☐ Automatically add new top-level pages to this menu

Display location ☐ Primary Navigation
☑ Secondary Navigation ←
☐ Mobile Navigation
☐ Topbar Navigation
☐ Footer Navigation

To see where that menu appears – go check your site!

After changes to the menu, make sure you click the 'Save Menu' button, which is usually at the bottom right hand corner and top right hand corner of the screen:

Save Menu

Adding a Page link to the Menu

To add pages to the menu, note that you already need to have created those pages.

Once they are created, go to *Pages > View All*.

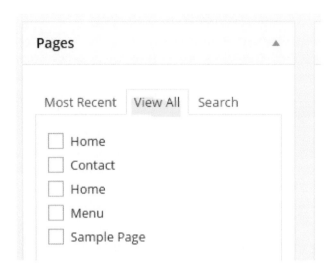

Now you will see a list of all the pages you have created.

To add them to the menu, simply select the box beside them (or 'Select All' to put all pages into the menu) and then click 'Add to Menu':

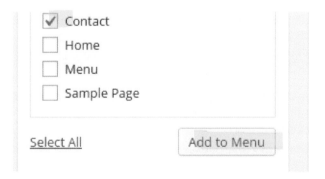

When you add a new page, it will automatically appear at the bottom of your menu. You can drag the menu blocks around to change the order. Home should always be first. 'Contact' should always be last.

To add a category you've made, scroll down and click 'Categories'.

To edit existing links in the menu, click on _____ of each item already in the menu.

Then you will see something like this;

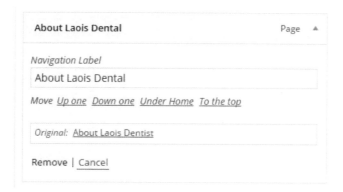

Note that the name of the link that appears in the navigation menu does not necessarily need to match the title of the page (which is the HTML h1 heading).

Change this by going to 'Navigation Label' and changing the text.

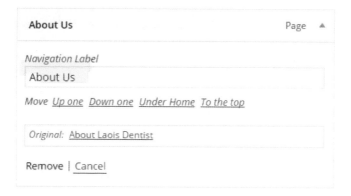

Generally, you would edit that field. Try to keep text in the Navigation links to one or two words – the heading on the top of each page can have more words.

Removing a Page from the Menu

To remove a link from a menu, click 'Remove'  - this removes the link to that page in the navigation menu.

Note that this doesn't actually delete the page – if you want to delte the page itself, you need to do that within 'Pages'

Submenus/Drop down menus

To add a 'submenu', simply drag the page by dragging and dropping with your mouse:

Contact	Custom ▾
Sample Page *sub item*	Page ▾

Now, 'Sample Page' is a subpage of 'Contact'

Check your theme, and, depending on the theme, ensure that when you hover over 'Contact' you see the dropdown/submenu appear.

You can create sub-submenus in the same way;

In the example above, 'Sample Page 2' and 'Sample Page 3' are in a menu off 'Sample Page', and 'Sample Page 4' is a sub-submenu, which the user reaches after hovering over 'Sample Page 3'.

Your theme may display a little down arrow, which indicates there is an

associated 'submenu':

Note: The appearance of your menu/submenu/sub-submenu etc. is predetermined in the theme.

Chapter 10: Creating a Gallery

First of all, don't bother reading this chapter unless it makes sense for you to build a gallery. If you want to put up generic pictures of stuff – maybe social media is the place for that. Don't bother making a gallery page unless it makes sense. Is it useful for your website visitors? Perhaps it is better for your website to keep a few excellent pictures throughout the different pages of the website?

A few years ago, you would have had to get a Plugin to create a gallery (you still can), but the WordPress inbuilt gallery is a nice place to start.

The first step is to go to *Pages > Add New.*

Where it says 'Enter title here', give the page the heading 1. I'm going to call my page here 'Gallery':

Add New Page

Enter title here

Click 'Add Media':

Add New Page

Gallery

Add Media   Visual Text Page Builder

Paragraph ▼ B I ≔ ≔ " ☰ ☰ ☰ 𝒫 ▤ ▦   ✕
ABE — A ▼ 🖹 ⊘ Ω ⊯ ⊯ ↰ ↱ ❓

On the left-hand side, click 'Create Gallery':

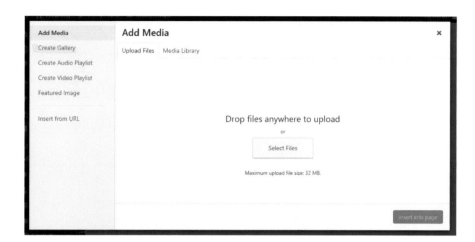

To upload files from your computer, click 'Select Files'

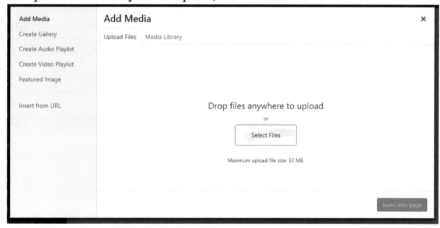

To add multiple files at a time, hold down the 'Ctrl' key on your keyboard if you use Windows, or 'Cmd' key if you use MAC.

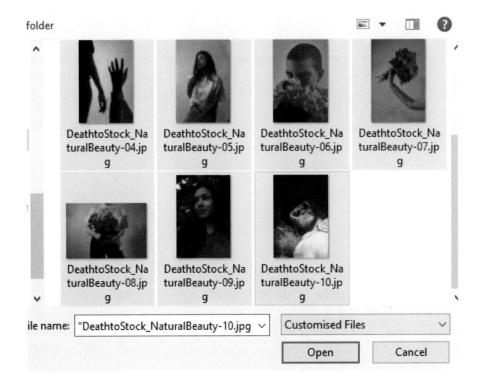

(By the way, the images I am using are from the old stock photography website, Death to Stock Photo, which, ironically, has now died. If you want free images to use then please see Images for your Site under Additional Resources at the end of this book).

If you have picked a few images, then you have to wait a while until all

of the images upload;

When the uploading is complete, you'll see that the images that you uploaded are all preselected:

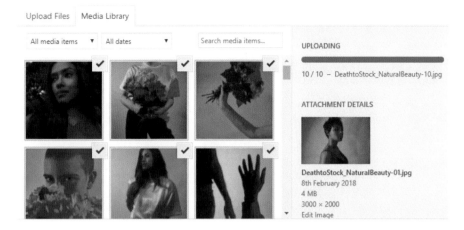

Click 'Create a new gallery' on the bottom right-hand side:

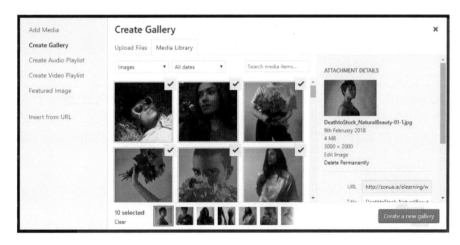

Add the gallery page to your website and then check to see how it looks. The appearance will vary based on the theme that you are using.

A lot of themes will display the pictures nicely, but, if you want some nicer effects (e.g. lightbox – which means that when the users clicks on the thumbnail picture, the large version will appear with the website in the background) – then you should get a gallery plugin. See Chapter 15: **Recommended Plugins** for some great plugins.

Chapter 11: Embedding Stuff

Embedding Google Maps

Full instructions here: » **www.zonua.ie/articles/embed-google-map.php**

Summary:

1. Get your business on Google maps by registering through »
    www.google.com/places

2. Click the menu icon ≡
    In the top left hand corner of your screen.

3. Click ⊖ Share or embed map

4. Select 'Embed map' – and copy and paste the code
    (corresponding to the blue code highlighted below):

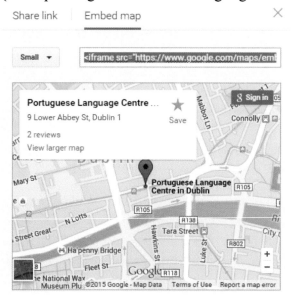

5. Copy the code and then paste it into your site, making sure to click 'Text' instead of 'Visual'

To centre your map, you need some HTML code. Remember that when you are putting code in, you need to select the 'Text Tab' instead of 'Visual':

1. Put this above your map code:

2. Put this at the end of your map code:

So the end result looks something like this:

Embedding YouTube Videos

1. Go the video you want to embed on YouTube

2. Click the Share icon:

3. Click 'Embed'

4. Deselect 'Show suggested videos when the video finishes;

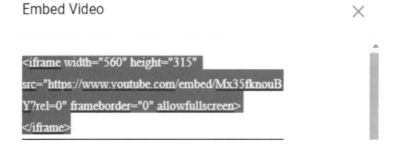

5. Copy the code like this;

Embed Video ✕

```
<iframe width="560" height="315"
src="https://www.youtube.com/embed/Mx35fknouB
Y?rel=0" frameborder="0" allowfullscreen>
</iframe>
```

6. Go to the relevant page on your website.

7. Click 'Text' instead of 'Visual'.

8. Paste in the code, save the page and check it!

Embedding a Facebook feed

To embed a Facebook feed;

1. Go to »
https://developers.facebook.com/docs/plugins/page-plugin

2. Put in the link to your Facebook page in the URL field, if you don't know the link, go and click on the full address in the address bar of your Facebook page. For example;

3. You don't have to specify the height or width. You might leave those fields empty – put them into your site, and then come back and edit if you don't like what you see. Ideally

if you have 'Adapt to plugin container width' then your widget will resize nicely.
However width of 240px is generally good width for the widget area in the sidebars.

4. To get the feed to appear: make sure 'timeline' is written in the 'Tabs' field

5. 'Use Small Header' and 'Hide Cover Photo' are optional

6. To get rid of the people's faces under the header section: unclick 'Show Friends' Faces'.

7. Finally, click [Get Code]

8. Unlike Twitter, YouTube or Google maps, where you just had to copy one piece of code, now you have to copy two pieces. Copy the first piece, and put it into your 'text' widget area that you want (as you would do with Twitter). Copy the second piece of code and then put that underneath the first part in your widget area.

Chapter 12: Virtue (Theme Specific)

Virtue is a free theme. It's a very popular free Wordpress theme, due to the versatility and the control that it gives. It's also e-commerce ready.

Note

You don't get the full available controls in Virtue until you install and activate the recommended plugin(s) in: *Appearance > Install Plugins*

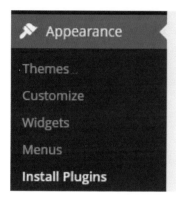

Logo

To upload your logo, go to: *Appearances > Theme Options > Main Settings > Logo Options*

Retina Logo -

Upload Your @2x Logo for Retina Screens

Should be twice the pixel size of your normal logo.

- This means, upload your logo at twice the size as your standard logo. E.g. if you uploaded a logo at 100px x 100px, make one that is 200px x 200px to upload here. This is for high-resolution screens such as the new iPhones.

Home Page in Virtue

First, you need to decide what elements appear on your homepage.

Set this in: *Appearance > Theme Options > Home Layout > Homepage Layout Manager.*

Whatever is in the 'Enabled Section' will appear on your homepage.

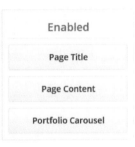

The order is relevant also.

e.g. in the above example, the Page Title will appear, then Content, and then the Portfolio Carousel.

Slideshow

To upload your logo, go to: *Appearance > Theme Options > Home Slider Settings.*

Recommended slideshow dimensions for Virtue are 1170pixels x 450pixels BUT if you want to use something different, you can change this:

Make sure you have one of the options in this dropdown selected for your slideshow to appear:

To add a new slide;

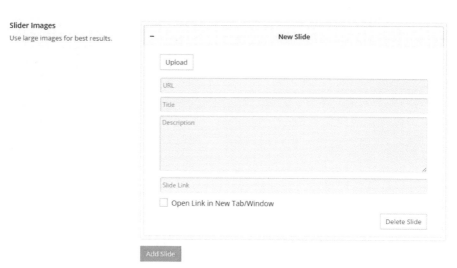

The Title, Description, Description and Slide Link are all optional.

I suggest use the Title for your text – the description text can get very small for mobiles. **Make sure you check this on a mobile phone.**

Link to relevant pages, where appropriate.

Slider for mobiles

If you want, you can have a separate slider for mobile phones; this might be where you might have a slideshow that has less pictures, or maybe pictures that you have specially selected for smaller screens. Remember to actually view your website on your mobile.

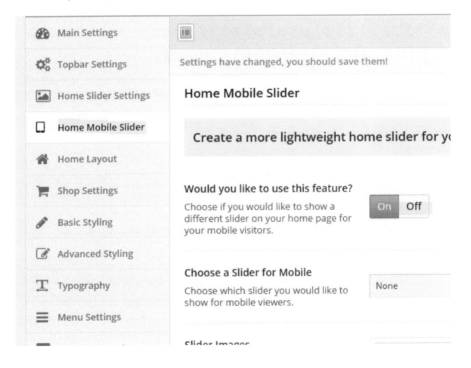

On the Homepage, note that 'Portfolio' refers to this:

Featured Projects

To get the portfolio carousel to appear, go to: *Appearances > Theme Options > Home Layout: Home Portfolio Carousel Settings ->* this is where you change the general settings.

The actual portfolio previews can only appear when you have created Portfolio pages:

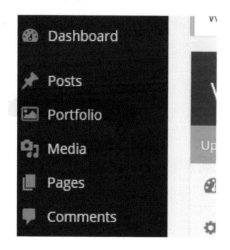

Note that the 'featured image' in the bottom right hand side is the image that will appear in the preview part on the homepage:

Featured Images on Blog

The image dimensions for the featured images on your blog are 335px x 335px in the Virtue theme.

Home Page in Virtue

First, you need to decide what elements appear on your homepage.

Set this in: *Appearance > Home Page.*

Ensure that you have this page 'Enabled' if you want to use this Custom

Home Page:

Here, you can add in different elements onto your homepage.

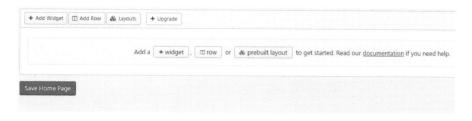

- Note the 'documentation' link: »
  https://siteorigin.com/page-builder/documentation - this
  page will help you with the layout of your homepage.

Slideshow

The slideshow that Virtue uses is called Meta Slider – you may need to
install this as a plugin if you haven't done so already.

To set the slideshow that you will use (it should be set at 'Meta Slider'),
go to: *Appearance > Customise > Theme Settings > Home*:

… change 'Demo Slider' to 'Meta Slider'

To upload your logo, go to: *Appearances > Theme Options > Home
Slider Settings.*

Vantage: Recommended slideshow dimensions for Vantage: 1080pixels
x 420pixels.

Meta Slider

This is a plugin that complements your theme, Vantage. To make a

slideshow, go to  in your Dashboard.

Click the '+' to add a new Slideshow, and then you can add new slides by clicking 'Add Slide':

Documentation on Meta Slider is here: »
https://www.metaslider.com/documentation/

Make sure you check this on a mobile phone.

Link to relevant pages, where appropriate.

Chapter 13: Vantage (Theme Specific)

Another very popular theme is Vantage. It's free. Due to i's popularity, I just wanted to briefly mention it here.

Note

You don't get the full available controls in Vantage until you install and activate the recommended plugin(s) in: *Appearance > Install Plugins*

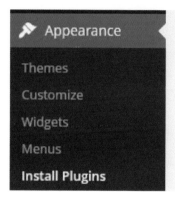

Logo

To upload your logo, go to: *Appearance > Customise > Theme Settings > Logo*.

There is no recommended size for your logo in the Vantage theme. However, for your reference, the logo size in the Vantage demo here: »
http://demo.siteorigin.com/vantage/ is 181px x 40px

Retina Logo:

Retina Logo

A double sized version of your logo for retina displays. Must be used in addition to standard logo.

No file selected

Select File

- This means, upload your logo at twice the size as your standard logo. E.g. if you uploaded a logo at 100px x 100px, make one that is 200px x 200px to upload here. This is for high-resolution screens such as the newer iPhones.

Chapter 14: Pinnacle (Theme Specific)

Note: Stuff in: *Appearance > Theme Options* overrides stuff in: *Appearance > Customize.*

Change background colours (e.g. footer colour): *Appearance > Theme Options > Advanced Styling*

Change background image on homepage: *Appearance > Theme Options > Home Slider >*

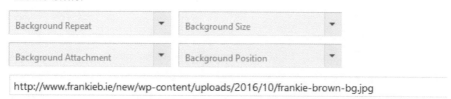

Upload favicon in: *Appearance > Theme Options > Misc Settings*

Change Main Menu text colour in: *Appearance > Theme Options > Site Header*

Menu Text Color (For Transparent Header)

Choose the font color of the menu font while background is transparent

Change Menu font types in: *Appearance > Theme Options > Menu Settings*

Change header background on all pages (apart from home): *Appearance > Theme Options > Page Title > Page Header Default Background*

Change h1 (heading 1) colour: *Appearance > Theme Options > Page Title > Page Title Colour*

Change h1 alignment: *Appearance > Theme Options > Page Title > Page Title Align*

Chapter 15: Plugins

Plugins are little pieces of pre-written code that can extend the functionality of your WordPress site.

To add in a Plugin, go to: *Plugins > Add New*:

Plugins need to be Installed **and** Activated.

How do I Know Which are the Best Plugins?

You are not the first person to make a site like this: This is the benefit of WordPress – learn from others' experiences

- Check the downloads.
- Check the star-rating

Literally: Google to see what other people are using! Also: ASK people what they are using. See the next section for some recommended plugins. If you need recommendations for anything more specific, ask me in the Facebook support group for this book: »
www.facebook.com/groups/WordPressMasterbook

You can also just keep reading and I've broken down the best plugins (in my opinion and experience) under different headings (like Speed or E-Commerce) in the section Recommended Plugins in Chapter 15.

How to Check What Version of WordPress You're Using

Some plugins only work with certain versions of WordPress. If you need to check what version of WordPress your are using, login to the Dashboard and scroll down to the bottom right-hand side of the screen, and you'll see something like this:

Version 5.0.3

                             - so, here, I can see I'm using Version 5.0.3 of WordPress.

Recommended Plugins

These are all free plugins via WordPress.org

SEO
- Google XML Sitemaps by Arne Brachold - **https://wordpress.org/plugins/google-sitemap-generator/**
- Yoast SEO by Team Yoast - **https://wordpress.org/plugins/wordpress-seo/**
- Google Analytics by MonsterInsights **https://wordpress.org/plugins/google-analytics-for-wordpress/**
- All in One SEO Pack by Micheal Torbert - **https://wordpress.org/plugins/all-in-one-seo-pack/**

Advanced SEO
- Schema App Structured Data by Hunch Manifest - **https://wordpress.org/plugins/schema-app-structured-data-for-schemaorg/**
- All In One Schema Rich Snippets by Brainstorm Force- **https://wordpress.org/plugins/all-in-one-schemaorg-rich-snippets/**
- WPSSO Schema JSON-LD Markup for Google Knowledge Graph, Merchant, Rich Card SEO, and Pinterest Rich Pins by JS Morisset - **https://wordpress.org/plugins/wpsso-schema-json-ld/**
- WPSSO Core – Complete Open Graph, Rich Pin, Twitter Card, SEO Meta Tags and Rich Results / Schema Markup by JS Morisset - **https://wordpress.org/plugins/wpsso**

Speed
- WP Super Cache by Automattic - **https://wordpress.org/plugins/wp-super-cache/**
- W3 Total Cache by Frederick Townes - **https://wordpress.org/plugins/w3-total-cache/**
- WP Fastest Cache by Emre Vona - **https://wordpress.org/plugins/wp-fastest-cache/**
- Smushit - **https://wordpress.org/plugins/wp-smushit/** - for image compression
- Imsanity - **https://wordpress.org/plugins/imsanity/**- resizes images to pre-determined sizes, especially useful for website where members/multiple users will be uploading pictures

Social Media & Contacting
- Contact Form 7 by Takayuki Miyoshi - **https://wordpress.org/plugins/contact-form-7/**
- Helios Solutions Social Media Buttons by Helios Solutions - **https://wordpress.org/plugins/hs-social-media-buttons/**
- Comments – wpDiscuz by gVectors Team - **https://wordpress.org/plugins/wpdiscuz/**
- Custom Feeds for Instagram by Smash Balloon: **https://wordpress.org/plugins/instagram-feed/**

Social Media Sharing
- Simple Share Button Adder by Simple Share Buttons - **https://wordpress.org/plugins/simple-share-buttons-adder/**
- WordPress Share Buttons, Related Posts, Google Analytics by Shareaholic - **https://wordpress.org/plugins/shareaholic/**

Newsletters
- Mailchimp for WordPress by ibericode: **https://wordpress.org/plugins/search/mailchimp/**
- MailPoet – emails and newsletters in WordPress by MailPoet - **https://wordpress.org/plugins/mailpoet/**

Backup & Security
- BackWPup WordPress Backup Plugin by Inspyde GmbH - **https://wordpress.org/plugins/backwpup/**
- iThemes Security by iThemes - **https://wordpress.org/plugins/better-wp-security/**
- Login LockDown by Mvandemar
- Limit Login Attempts Reloaded by WPChef - **https://wordpress.org/plugins/limit-login-attempts-reloaded/**
- Wordfence Security – Firewall & Malware Scan by Wordfence - **https://wordpress.org/plugins/wordfence/**

SSL

- Really Simple SSL by Rogier Lankhorst - **https://wordpress.org/plugins/really-simple-ssl/**
  - You need this if you've just moved your website from http to https, as you need to change all the internal links (including pictures, css) to https instead of http – this plugin does it for you in a matter of seconds.

GDPR, Cookie Policy & Legal Stuff
- GDPR Cookie Consent Banner by termly - **https://wordpress.org/plugins/uk-cookie-consent/**

- I love this plugin. It automatically makes a Cookies Policy page for you (which you can modify further if you wish)
  - Modify in Settings > Cookie Consent -
- GDPR Cookie Consent by WebToffee - **https://wordpress.org/plugins/cookie-law-info/**
- GDPR by Trew Knowledge - **https://wordpress.org/plugins/gdpr/**

Advanced/Techy Stuff
- GeoIP Detection by Yellow Tree - **https://wordpress.org/plugins/geoip-detect/**
- Head, Footer & Post Injections by Stefano Lissa - **https://wordpress.org/plugins/header-footer/** - this plugin is great for putting code into the header, e.g. Google Analytics or the Facebook pixel tracking code.

E-Commerce
- WooCommerce Mailchimp by Adam Anderly
- Enhanced Ecommerce Google Analytics Plugin for WooCommerce by Tatvic - **https://wordpress.org/plugins/enhanced-e-commerce-for-WooCommerce-store/**

Booking Engines
- This plugin is created for salons, but could be used by any business who needs to take appointments (e.g. personal trainer, doctor) – Salon Booking System by WordPress Chef - **https://wordpress.org/plugins/salon-booking-system/**

Tables
- Tablepress by TobiasBg - **https://wordpress.org/plugins/tablepress/**
- For a Restaurant Menu: Restaurant Menu by MotoPress - **https://wordpress.org/plugins/mp-restaurant-menu/**
- Ninja Tables – Best WP Data Table Plugin for WordPress by WPManageNinja LLC - **https://wordpress.org/plugins/ninja-tables/**

Calendars
- Event Calendar WD – Responsive Event Calendar by WebDorado - **https://wordpress.org/plugins/spider-event-calendar/**

Galleries
- Photo Gallery by WD – Responsive Photo Gallery for WordPress by Photo Gallery Team - **https://wordpress.org/plugins/photo-gallery/**
- Pixproof by Pixelgrade – Allows you to have a password-protected area for different galleries - **https://wordpress.org/plugins/pixproof/**
- Gallery by Envira – Responsive Photo Gallery for WordPress by Envira Gallery Team - **https://wordpress.org/plugins/envira-gallery-lite/**

Multilingual stuff
- Virtue theme is already an approved WordPress theme that will integrate well with this plugin. For Virtue, see here: **http://www.kadencethemes.com/working-wpml/**
- Loco Translate by Tim Whitlock is also really handy for translating a word here or there (for example an inbuilt word in your theme): **https://wordpress.org/plugins/loco-translate/**

- *Alert! This is the only paid-for plugin recommended in this book*: WPML: **https://wpml.org/** The WordPress Multilingual Plugin is very popular and very good.

Various:
- Duplicate Post – clone existing pages and posts - **https://wordpress.org/plugins/duplicate-post/**

Page Builders

If you want to do something like using parallax sections on your website, have columns or 'thirds' on your website, then a Page Builder is a good idea. A Page Builder replaces the standard Editor in WordPress.

Note that these Gutenberg is not included in these recommendations!

- Page Builder by SiteOrigin by SiteOrigin (not a typo!) - **https://wordpress.org/plugins/siteorigin-panels/**
- Elementor Page Builder by Elementor.com - **https://wordpress.org/plugins/elementor/**
- Classic Editor by WordPress Contributors – activate this plugin to use the 'old' WordPress Editor instead of Gutenberg: **https://wordpress.org/plugins/classic-editor/**

Google Analytics

To get Google Analytics to work on your site, you first need to sign up with Google Analytics and then you will get a 'UA' code, which is simply a code beginning with 'UA' – something like UA-123457855-1

After installing the plugin, Google Analytics by Monster Insights, go to 'Settings'.

103

You can follow the instructions to verify automatically, or, to do it manually: paste in your UA-code like this;

☑ **Manually enter your UA code**   UA-123457855-1|

Hit 'Save Changes' at the bottom of the page when done. Now Google Analytics can track the visitors to your website.

See towards the end of this document for instructions on how to sign up with Google Analytics.

Social Media Link Buttons – (i.e. links to your profiles)

- Floating Social Media Icon by Acurax

Once installed, you'll see this appear towards the bottom of your menu

on the right hand side;

Then, fill in whatever link that you want to appear on the site;

e.g. if I only fill in this field;

Twitter Username: zonua

Facebook Page/Profile URL:

Google Plus URL:

Pinterest URL:

Youtube URL:

Linkedin URL:

Feed URL:

- Then Twitter is the only icon that will appear

Contact Form

- Contact Form 7 by Takayuki Miyoshi

Once installed, you'll see this in your menu, to edit the Contact Forms;

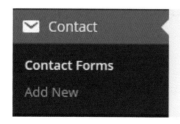

Once you make the Contact form, remember to paste the 'short code' onto the page where you want the form to appear;

☐ Contact form 1   [contact-form-7 id="84" title="Contact form 1"]
   Edit   Duplicate

Always test your Contact Form. If you do a tiny typo in your email address, you won't get the emails – and people will think you are ignoring their mails!

Comment Forms for Blogs

- I like Disqus. You need to sign up with disqus.com as well as install the Disqus plugin.

eCommerce Plugin

- The best **has** to be WooCommerce by WooThemes

Looking for something more basic? Try the Simple WordPress PayPal Shopping Cart Plugin

Fix broken links by Fedirecting

- Get the 'Redirection' plugin by John Godley; - https://wordpress.org/plugins/redirection/

You *need* to learn about redirections if you are;

a) Redeveloping a new website on an old domain (e.g. making a new website that will be on the same domain as before)
b) Deleting Pages
c) Renaming the URLs in pages, after they have been indexed by Google

Limit Login Attempts

WordPress is probably the most popular CMS system in the world. Unfortunately, it's popularity makes it extremely attractive to hackers. The default in WordPress is that login attempts aren't limited, which means that your site is vulnerable to brute-force attacks. This is when a hacker can run a programme that can keep trying to login to your WordPress account, until it gets the right username-password combination. Get Limit Login Attempts by Johanee/Johan Eenfeldt, a super simple plugin, which allows you to limit the login attempts. So, if the password is put in (for example) three times in a row incorrectly, no login attempts will be accepted for a certain amount of time that you specify.

Edit these settings in 'Limit Login Attempts' under the 'Settings' heading in your menu;

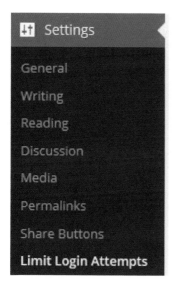

Backing Up Your Site

A great plugin, that is easy to use, to back-up both the files AND the database is:

'BackWPup' – this is a plugin. Install it and activate it, and then follow the instructions on

» **www.zonua.ie/articles/WordPress-backup.php**

The first thing you need to know is that the width of the images should be 360px. You decide the height. This means that you can choose, for example, 360px for the height – and then each image should be 360px in height, so that they look uniform. Or, if you choose 400px, then every other image in the carousel should also be 400px.

1. Upload the image to: *Media > Add New*

2. Go to: Media > Library
   a. Click on the image you uploaded, and copy the URL – this is the link of the image.

Tip: Ctrl+A = copy all. Ctrl+C = copy. Ctrl+P = paste

To modify this slider, go to *Carousel Slider > Add New* in the dashboard menu;

If you want to add in an image, text, and link, set 'Slide Type' as 'Image Carousel – from URL':

Image Carousel Test

Carousel Slider

Slide Type

Image Carousel - from URL ▾

URL Images

Images URLs
Enter external images URLs.

Edit URLs

Image Carousel Settings

Then, click Edit, and a box like this appears:

URL = link of the image. This means that you must upload the image BEFORE you actually make this carousel.

Title = Title text

Caption = text underneath the title

Alt Text = alternative text for the image, good for SEO

Link to URL = page that you want to link to

Then, go to Appearance > Widgets, and bring the Carousel Slider to the widget area.

E.g. it would look like this:

Image Carousel Test

| title | title | title |
| caption | caption | caption |

Widgets

Generally speaking, a widget is a plugin that **appears** on your website. To check the Widgets that are already installed, go to: *Appearance > Widgets*.

On the left-hand side, you can see the 'Available Widgets'. These are widgets that are already installed. Some come preinstalled with WordPress, some come preinstalled with your theme. Then you can install others yourself.

On the right-hand side of your page, you can see where you drag the Widgets to appear on your website. Depending on your theme, you might have sections called 'Right Sidebar', 'Sidebar', 'Footer Area One'.

If you are not sure which is which, then drag anything into one of them (e.g. 'Calendar'), and then check your website to see where it has appeared. Make sure you hit 'Save' when you drag in or update a Widget:

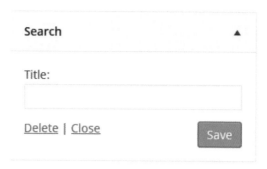

The 'Text' Widget is one of the most useful, since you can do anything with this.

This is also where we can add in HTML. So, for example, you can put in your Google maps code here, embed a YouTube video, or even the Twitter feed widget code that you get from Twitter.

If you have an idea for a widget, and don't have it in the options on the left hand side under 'Available Widgets', then you can either figure out how to do it in the 'Text' widget, or, changes are – someone has already made what you want as a plugin. When you install and activate a plugin that is a widget, then you'll automatically see it in the 'Widgets' page under 'Available Widgets'.

Updating Plugins

Most popular plugins get updated regularly; the system will tell you when there's an update available. You'll see something like this;

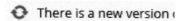

You can check by going to: *Plugins > Update Available*

To update, simply hit the `update now.` button.

You don't need to update every single time there's an update. Sometimes you'll see text that tells you there's been quite a big update and you should update. However you might decide to update twice a year.

N.B. Back up your whole WordPress website before you do an update.

After an update, check whatever that plugin did (e.g. if it was a Social Media Share button, check that they still work).

Remember: Plugins always need to be Installed and Activated before you can get them to work on your site.

If you haven't updated in a long time, it's best to update plugins one-by-one, so that you can check your site after each update. To do this, go to Plugins, and you'll immediately see which plugins have an available update, for example, here, there's an update available for 'Classic Editor' but not 'BackWPup':

BackWPup

Deactivate

WordPress Backup Plugin

Version 3.6.7 | By Inpsyde GmbH | View details | Documentation

Classic Editor

Deactivate | Settings

Enables the WordPress classic editor and the old-style Edit Post screen with TinyMCE, Meta Boxes, etc. Supports the older plugins that extend this screen.

Version 1.3 | By WordPress Contributors | View details

There is a new version of Classic Editor available. View version 1.4 details or update now.

To update the Classic Editor, it couldn't be easier – click on the 'update now' link:

> ↻ There is a new version of Classic Editor available. View version 1.4 details or update now.

After updating;

> ↻ Updating...

you'll see a message like this:

> ✓ Updated!

and that's it – done!

Chapter 16: SEO

SEO and WordPress

SEO means Search Engine Optimisation, which is all about your website being found, understood and ranked in search engines like Google, Yahoo, Bing, DuckDuckGo, Yandex etc.

WordPress is probably the best CMS option for SEO.

While this isn't an 'SEO book', it's important to at least mention SEO here. If you think about SEO at the start – while making your website – it makes your life much easier, than retrospectively coming back to change it.

Some parts of SEO are super simple, some parts of SEO are very technical. However, if you want to simplify SEO right down, then, while making your website, you should be think about **text** and **links**. From the text point of view – if you want to rank highly for certain search terms, then your content needs to reflect that. Get your search terms into your text.

Some quick SEO tips
- Get your search terms into your headings
- Get your search terms as high up the page as possible (e.g. the first sentence of the first paragraph)
- Get your search terms into the links
- Rename your images with your search terms before you upload them to your website
- Set the alt and the title of the images.
- Internal links are important (e.g. if, on the About page, you write 'please contact us' - make that be a link to the Contact page.)

- Speed is important: The faster your page appears on my screen, the happier I will be, but also, *the happier Google will be,* and the better you will rank.

> **"The faster your page appears the better you will rank"**

When it comes to SEO plugins for WordPress, you really have two choices;

- All in One SEO Pack by Micheal Torbert
- Yoast SEO by Team Yoast

Both have very good reviews, I prefer Yoast SEO by Team Yoast, which is also more popular with over 5 million active installs, versus over three million active installs for All in One SEO Pack.

Yoast SEO by Team Yoast

Once installed, click into 'Pages' and you'll see some extra headings appear;

Click into any page.

Scroll down and you'll see a section that looks like this towards the bottom of the page;

The SEO title is the blue text that appears in search listings.

The Meta description is the black/dark grey text that appears in search listings.

Control how your page listing looks in the search engines
In the section 'WordPress SEO by Yoast' at the bottom of each page, you can edit the title and description. These control how your blog listing may appear in Google/Bing:

Click 'Edit Snippet' to edit the SEO title and meta description.

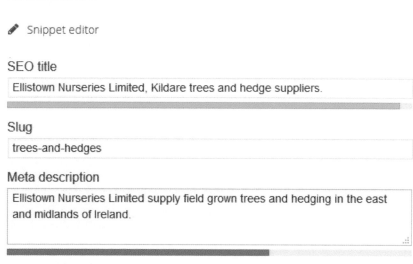

Ellistown Nurseries Limited, Kildare trees and hedge suppliers.

ellistownnurseries.com/new/trees-and-hedges/

Ellistown Nurseries Limited supply field grown trees and hedging in the east and midlands of Ireland.

✎ Snippet editor

SEO title

Ellistown Nurseries Limited, Kildare trees and hedge suppliers.

Slug

trees-and-hedges

Meta description

Ellistown Nurseries Limited supply field grown trees and hedging in the east and midlands of Ireland.

Close snippet editor

Click 'Close snippet editor' once done.

Note that it takes Google a few days to recognise these changes.

Test which page is more effective for site visitors in Behavior > Experiments. Test very subtle differences, to improve your conversion rate.

How to sign up with Google Analytics.

1. Sign up at » **https://analytics.google.com** If you don't see a page like this when you login . . .

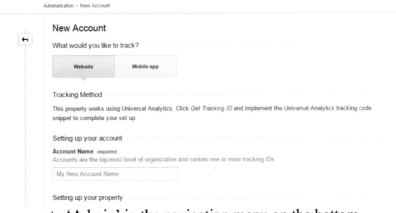

. . . . go to 'Admin' in the navigation menu on the bottom left hand side of your screen:

. . . . click 'Account'

ACCOUNT

Click 'Create New Account':

Create new account

2. Put your domain in each of these fields;

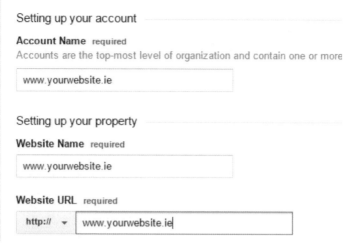

3. Industry Category doesn't matter too much – select whatever is closest to what you do.

4. Change the country and timezone to whatever makes sense for you;

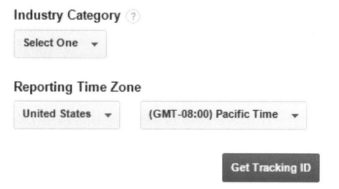

5. At the bottom of the page, click

6. Then the next screen will ask you to agree to the T&Cs. Do so.

7. Then on the next page you will see a 'UA' code. That just means a code beginning with 'UA'. Write it down/email it to yourself. This is the verification code we need to put Google Analytics on our websites.

Google Analytics;

I've put together the five most important things you should be checking regularly within Google Analytics.

1. Check a general overview: *Audience > Overview*

2. Check where your traffic is coming from: *Acquisition > Overview*

3. Know the most important pages on your site: *Behaviour > Site Content > All Pages*

4. Look at the timelines: Daily, Weekly, Monthly (change in the top right-hand corner of any page)

5. Are people coming from desktops or mobiles? Check in *Audience > Mobile > Overview*

Advanced Stuff

- For e-commerce sites, use Google Analytics to track conversions: *Settings > Account > View Settings*: Turn 'Ecommerce tracking' on.
- Set up Alerts in Intelligence Events to get alerts by text/email.

Example of Cookies Policy for Google Analytics

The only cookies in use on our site are for **Google Analytics**. Google Analytics is a web analytics tool that helps website owners understand how visitors engage with their website. Google Analytics customers can view a variety of reports about how visitors interact with their website so that they can improve it.

Like many services, Google Analytics uses first-party cookies to track visitor interactions as in our case, where they are used to collect information about how visitors use our site. We then use the information to compile reports and to help us improve our site.
Cookies contain information that is transferred to your computer's hard drive. These cookies are used to store information, such as the time that the current visit occurred, whether the visitor has been to the site before and what site referred the visitor to the web page.

Google Analytics collects information anonymously. It reports website trends without identifying individual visitors. **You can opt out of Google Analytics without affecting how you visit our site** – for more information on opting out of being tracked by Google Analytics across all websites you use, visit this Google page.
(link is here: » **https://tools.google.com/dlpage/gaoptout**)

Chapter 17: Users

I always found it interesting that the website industry is one of the only two industries I can think of, where the people who keep the industry surviving (and thriving) are called 'users'.

You are automatically an Administrator on your WordPress site. This means you have full access to edit your website, upload pages, change the theme, upload WordPress etc.

If you want to give someone else access to your WordPress site, you should not give them your login details, but rather make them their own account.

To add a new User, go to: *Users > Add New:*

The username needs to be unique, and cannot be changed. The email also needs to be unique (i.e. one username per email address).

The role depends on the access you want to give the user. It's best to only give access to people to the areas they need. For example, if you have someone who will only update the blog section on their website, you don't need to give them access to change the theme.

In this case, you should make them an 'Editor' and not 'Administrator':

This both keeps things more simple for them (they'll only see the options that they can edit, and so, a more simple Dashboard), and it controls who can change your website.

If someone makes your WordPress website for you, but you find you cannot change the theme, or update plugins, then you probably only have 'Editor' access. The main Administrator needs to be contacted, to change your account from Editor to Administrator;

See the list of Users in: *Users > All Users*.

Sometimes you might have pages on your website that you only want certain clients to have access to, for example, a photographer might only want to give a client access to a gallery of an event. If you install a plugin, you may see the users automatically have a 'subscriber' account or similar.

Chapter 18: E-Commerce

This section concentrates solely on WooCommerce, which is the most popular plugin for implementing e-commerce on a WordPress website. If you want to accept payments on your website, if you want stock control and to be able to keep track of orders and to offer discounts – you should get WooCommerce.

Note: This chapter covers the most basic elements that you need to know when setting up an e-commerce website. If you need more help, see the Additional Resources *at the end of this book.*

It makes your life much easier if you begin by picking a theme that is compatible with WooCommerce.

WooCommerce allows stock control, automated emails to customers, creation of vouchers and much more.

To Install WooCommerce, go to: *Plugins > Add New.*

Once installed and activated, you will notice two new sections in the main menu area of your WordPress website:

The WooCommerce section controls the main 'overall' settings for your WooCommerce website:

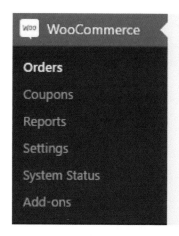

The 'Products' section is similar to 'Pages' or 'Posts'. Each product on your website will have its own Product page.

Product Type Explanation

Before you begin adding a product, you should decide what type it is;

Simple Product

According to WooCommerce, this is the most common type of product. A simple product is one that has no options related to it – for example a book, a bottle of wine. The product is sold as-is.

Variable Product

This is the most time-consuming type of product. You will need to set up a variable product if your product has options – for example a t-shirt that comes in different sizes, or a candle that comes in different scents. Variable products can have various options, for example a t-shirt could be sold in three different sizes (e.g. S, M and L), and in two different colours (e.g. Yellow and Green) – in which case you have six different options on the one product page.

Virtual Product

You would set up a Virtual Product if you are selling something that will not be shipped or posted. For example, a consultation or service.

Downloadable Product

If you are selling a file, for example an MP3 track or a PDF ebook, then you would use Downloadable Product. After purchase, the customer can automatically download the file.

Add a Product

After giving the product a title (remember that the title in WordPress is the heading1, and from an SEO perspective, it is good to get your search terms here), you will start adding the content to the page.

First, add some text in the main content section and note where it appears:

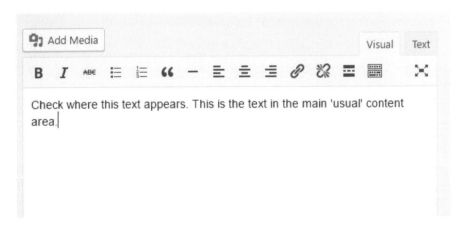

For the vast majority of themes, the short description will actually appear above the main description.

For example;

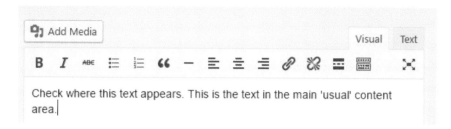

and

could produce this;

So, in this case, the 'Short Description' is actually more important for customers visiting this page.

Images

The Product Image (e.g. the picture in the example above) gets set in the 'Product Image' section towards the bottom right hand side of your screen;

This section: may or may not get shown, depending on the theme you are using.

Adding a Simple Product

A simple product is one that has no variations. This means it is sold as shown -for example, customers cannot choose different sizes of the product.

Specific product data (e.g. price, weight, stock) is set and controlled in the 'Product Data' section:

Note the different tabs on the right-hand side;

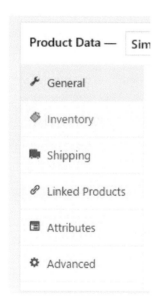

In the 'General', you can set the price of your product.

If you have a sale on, you can set a 'Sale price':

Regular price (€)	40
Sale price (€)	30

You can schedule the sale to start and end on specific dates;

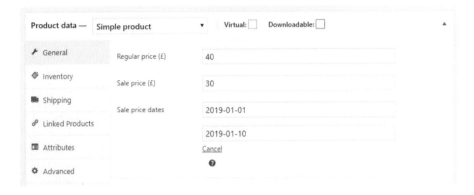

In the 'Inventory' tab, you can control the stock;

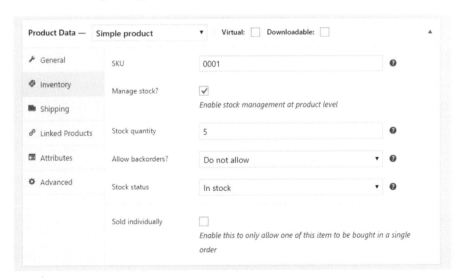

The SKU is the Stock-Keeping-Unit, and although it is not necessary, and just a reference for you, it is a good practice to implement a SKU system to monitor your stock. The SKU can be shown on the front-end of the website, which means that customers can see it. In certain cases, this could be useful for customers when enquiring about a product that is very similar to another.

Tick the 'Manage stock?' box to enable stock management.

The 'Stock quantity' level is the amount of stock of that product. You can manually increase or decrease that number whenever you sell that product offline, suffer a breakage, or get new stock.

The 'Stock quantity' will automatically decrement when the product is sold via your website.

'Allow backorders' – if this is selected it means that customers can choose to buy the product even if it is not in stock. In this case, customers will see some text that it is currently not in stock, and you should contact them after the purchase to let them know when to expect the product.

Note that 'Stock status' overrides the 'Stock quantity', so, even if you have 'Stock quantity' as 5, but 'Stock Status' as 'Not in stock' - the website will show the product as out of stock.

'Sold individually' means that customers can buy nothing else in the same purchase as this order. Note that this would typically not be selected, but it could make sense in some circumstances for you to select this to avoid customer error.

Adding a Downloadable Product

Firstly, check *WooCommerce > Settings > Products > Downloadable Products*:

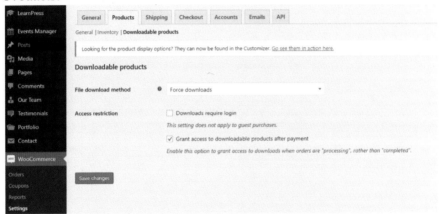

- the default is shown above, and probably makes sense for you too.

Next, go to Products > Add New, and add a new Simple Product, as in the previous section. This time, select 'Downloadable' like this;

You will then see the section below appear, where you can click 'Add File' to upload the file;

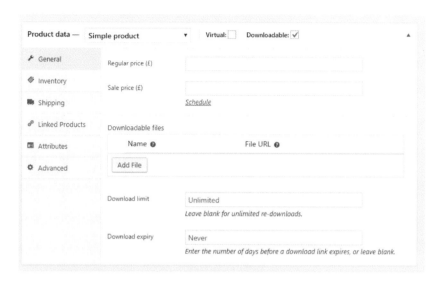

You can set a limit on the amount of downloads the user can make (it probably makes most sense for you to lave that blank for unlimited re-downloads), and you can set the expiry date for when the download link will expire.

Adding a Variable Product

Begin by adding your product, and in the 'Product Data' section, select 'Variable product' from the dropdown;

Product data — Variable product ▼

Click 'Attributes':

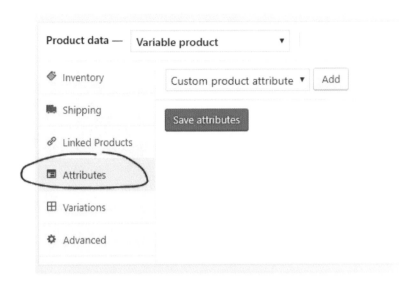

Add your attributes.

To use a 'global attribute': Select one from the dropdown and Add.

Choose Select all to add all attributes to the variable product (if applicable).

To add custom attributes, specific to that product;

a) Select Custom product attribute from the dropdown;

b) Click 'Add'

c) Name the attribute (e.g. Size or Colour)

d) Set values separated by a vertical pipe (e.g., Small | Medium | Large)
   Note: on my keyboard, the pipe icon can be found on with Shift + Backspace key

e) Enable the Used for variations checkbox.

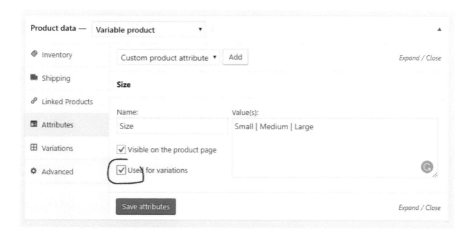

f) Click 'Save attributes'

g) Next, click 'Variations':

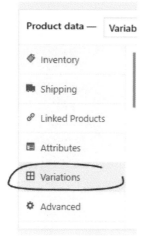

Select 'Create variations from all attributes' from the dropdown menu and click 'Go';

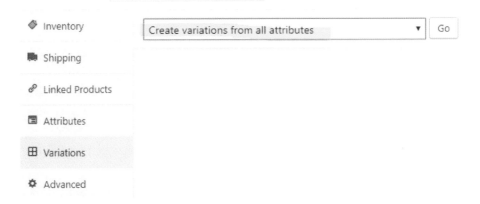

A message like this will appear;

Are you sure you want to link all variations? This will create a new variation for each and every possible combination of variation attributes (max 50 per run).

OK   Cancel

Click 'OK'.

Click 'Expand' to see the different settings;

Edit any available data.

*The only **required** field is Regular Price.* Some people think it's a bit counter-intuitive, but you **must** set the 'Regular Price' for each variation, even if all of the variations cost the same.

Click;

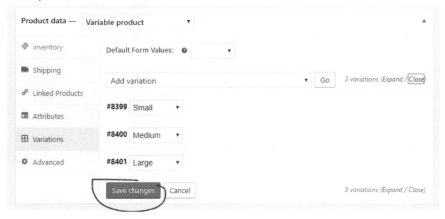

You then need to click the usual 'Publish' button to save the whole page, before you see it appear in your shop.

Importing Bulk Products

Advanced Alert! This section is not for beginners, and is for more adventurous and ambitions WordPress users!

For best understanding, you should manually add and edit products (as in the previous sections) before attempting this bulk method.

If you have many products to upload at the one time, you can use a .CSV file and then bulk import. The CSV file has to have a special format. If you are using this method for the first time, then you should manually upload some products to your website, ensure they are exactly as you want, and then export the CSV from your website. (See: Exporting Existing Products from the Website)

This section assumes you have your CSV file ready to upload.

Steps Involved When Importing a CSV:

1. Add product data to the table

2. Resize the picture for each product to be the right size for your website (e.g. 1000px x 1000px)

3. Rename this file to have search terms in the file name, e.g. diamond-ring.jpg or silver-and-gold-ted-baker-earrings.jpg

4. Copy and paste the file name into the 'image' column of your CSV file.

5. Go to your WordPress dashboard, click on *Media > Add New*, and add this image.
   Note: You can add multiple images.

6. Double-check the CSV file, especially:
   - Product Category: if you are not sure about the Product Category, go to your WordPress dashboard, and select *Products > Category* and there you can see all categories previously made.
   - Image: the file-name has to be exactly correct.
   - Variable & Variation information.

7. Go to *Tools > Import > WooCommerce products (CSV) > Run Importer*:

WooCommerce products (CSV)   Import products to your store via a csv file.
Run Importer

8. Upload your CSV file from your computer:

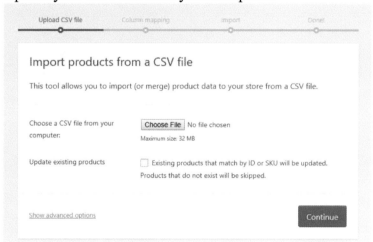

9. Check to make sure all the fields are allocated properly, e.g. column name 'ID' is mapped to field 'ID', 'Type' is mapped to 'Type' and so on, like this:

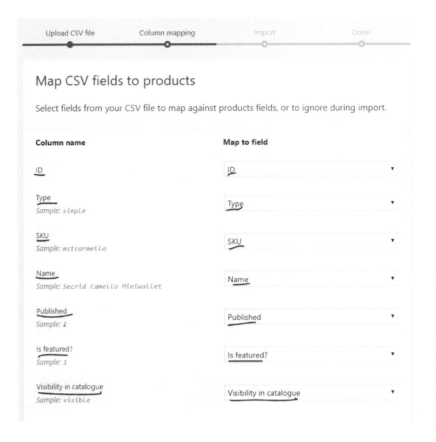

10. When everything is checked, click 'Run the Importer':

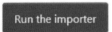

and you'll get a message that looks like this:

When the importer is complete, you'll get a message like this:

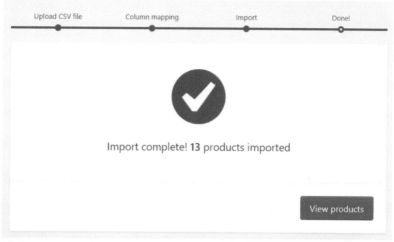

If there were any issues with the importer, a message will tell you same.

11. Go to Products in your Dashboard and check that things look right – i.e. that the products are there, with the correct picture(s) and details.

12. Go to your live website and check that things look right!

Exporting Existing Products from the Website

You may want to do this to check the existing settings on products that are already on your website. This is an especially good idea if you haven't bulk-imported products in long time, and want to remind yourself what is required on your website.

Go to Products in the Dashboard menu, and at the top of the page, click 'Export' – you can then download a .csv file of your products.

Discount Codes

To set up a discount code, or coupon, for your WooCommerce website go to *WooCommerce > Coupons > Add coupon.*

You'll then arrive on a page that looks like this;

- You can limit the amount of times the coupon gets used.
- You can set a voucher that only works for certain products.
- You can set a voucher that only works for certain categories.
- You can set a voucher that only works for cost amounts over a certain amount.
- You can block the voucher for usage against certain products or categories.
- You can set a free shipping code.

Disabling Coupons in WooCommerce

Sometimes website owners know that they will never offer a discount, and I get asked how to disable the 'Enter Coupon Code' field on checkout.

To hide the field, go to *WooCommerce > Settings > General,* and deselect this box;

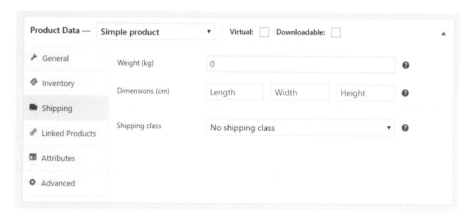

Shipping and Delivery Costs

If you charge delivery by weight or size of the product, you can fill in the weight/dimensions on the individual product pages;

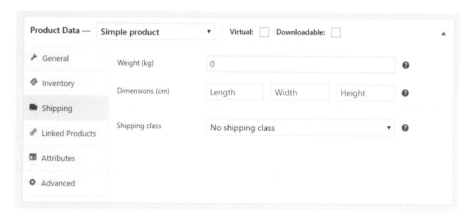

You can further change the shipping settings in: *WooCommerce > Settings > Shipping* – which is the standard way of doing things.

There are loads of ways to set up the shipping/delivery. I'm going to show you what most of my clients ask for – free shipping over a certain amount, with different rates for outside your own country:

Free Shipping Over a Certain Amount for One Country
Go to *WooCommerce > Settings > Shipping*.

First, in Shipping Zones, click 'Add Shipping Zone':

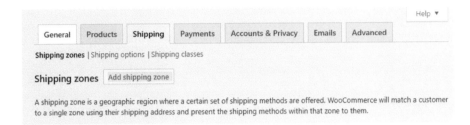

Give your Zone a name. Below, I'm going to create a zone for Germany, so I'm going to call my zone 'Germany'. Note, that this is just a reference for you, you need to further specify what your zone is referring to, in the second field, 'Zone regions': So, in this case, I need to select 'Germany' from the drop-down list.

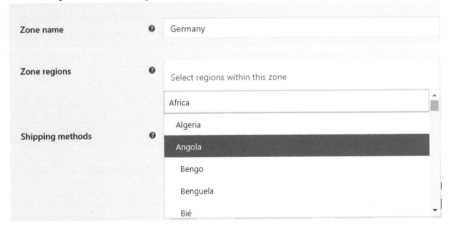

You can select multiple 'Zone Regions' by holding down the alt key on your keyboard.

Next, add a 'Shipping Method':

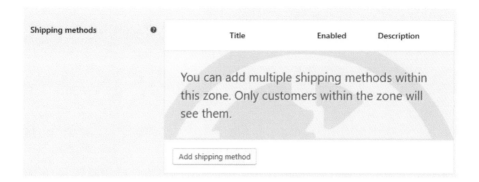

Once you click 'Add Shipping Method', this pop-up will appear;

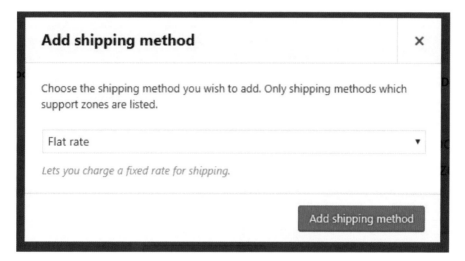

Flat rate means that a fixed price will apply for all purchases to the region you have previously defined.

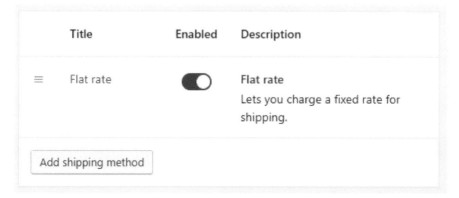

Once you add the 'Flat Rate', click on the words 'Flat Rate', and set the extra cost for shipping that you'll charge, e.g. here, my website visitors will pay €10 for delivery to Germany (the zone I've earlier selected).

Click 'Save changes'.

Often, e-commerce websites will allow free shipping over a certain amount, e.g. if I spend €100 or more on your website, then I get free shipping. You can set this up, after you have the 'flat rate' set:

Click 'Add shipping Method';

<table>
<tr><td></td><td>Title</td><td>Enabled</td><td>Description</td></tr>
<tr><td>≡</td><td>Flat rate</td><td>⬤</td><td>Flat rate
Lets you charge a fixed rate for shipping.</td></tr>
<tr><td colspan="4">Add shipping method</td></tr>
</table>

In the dropdown, select 'Free shipping';

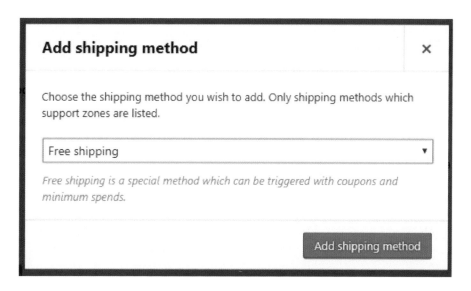

Here, I've set it up so that if anyone spends €100 or more on my website, they will get free shipping. (If someone spends less than €100, they will be charged the €10 for shipping).

Free shipping Settings

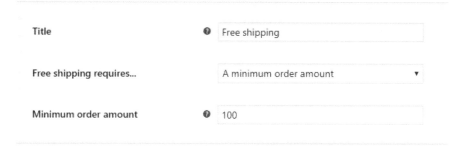

As you can see, you can set up as many shipping zones as you want, so you could offer different shipping rates to different countries (e.g. USA), or different regions (e.g. Europe).

The most popular payment method for new websites is PayPal.

PayPal has a number of advantages over other options including;

- It's free – you don't need to pay a subscription
- If you sell nothing, you pay nothing to PayPal
- It's a recognisable brand – so, potential customers who haven't heard of will feel they can trust PayPal.
- It's easy to set up
- You don't need a separate bank account to be integrated with PayPal.

It's incredibly easy to connect PayPal to WooCommerce. After creating your PayPal business account;

1. Go to *WooCommerce > Settings*, and then, across the menu at the top, go to *Checkout > PayPal*:

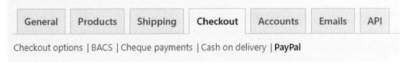

2. Make sure you have enabled PayPal Standard;

3. Where it says 'PayPal email' – enter the email address that you have set up with PayPal;

4. Down the bottom of the page, click Save changes

That's it!

Advanced PayPal Settings

You don't have to set up an API, but it's a good idea (if I was paying a developer, I would expect to have this done).

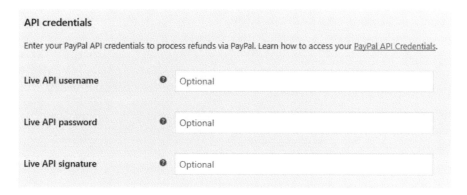

To get the API username, password and signature, log on to your PayPal Business Account. Note: I said 'Business' – not 'Personal'.

1. Click Profile, on the top right-hand side: {⚙} Profile
2. Click {⚙} Profile and settings
3. Click 'My selling tools'

4. Click 'Update' in the 'API access' row;

API access   Manage API credentials to integrate my PayPal account with   Update
                    my online store or shopping cart.

5. Click 'Grant API permission'

How is PayPal set up on your website?

 PayPal API

Through a shopping cart provider

Pre-built payment solution

If you're using or plan to use a 3rd-party platform, like Magento or Shopify, for shopping carts and online stores where the PayPal payment processor is built in.

Grant API permission, or Manage API permission

6. Click 'Manage PayPal Checkout settings';

Accept or block payments from your online stores before setting up APIs.

To begin using APIs, you first need to accept or block payments from your stores.
You can set up API permissions or credentials later.

Manage PayPal Checkout settings

Styling the Custom Payment Pages

Login to PayPal, and then put this link into the address bar in your browser: **https://www.paypal.com/cgi-bin/customerprofileweb?cmd=_profile-page-styles**

Chapter 19: Speed

Great resource: http://www.dwuser.com/education/content/10-steps-to-a-faster-WordPress/

As speed is now more important than ever, I've decided to dedicate a whole chapter to speed.

Things That Could Effect Speed

- Unused Plugins
- Unnecessary Plugins (plugin bloat is a major cause of slow site performance)
- Images are too large
- Advertisements
- Using a CDN Network
- Advertisements (e.g. if you allow external ads on your website, e.g. if you have signed up to Adsense and allow Google ads from third parties on your website)

Case Study: Which Plugin Best Increased Speed

In 2018, I tested a website using three different free plugins on a website.

Website Information
- Host: Blacknight
- Theme: Virtue Premium

Here, I will share the results with you.

There are numerous tests out there to measure the page speed of your website. Some people will recommend different tests to you. However, assuming your customers are based in a part of the world where Google is dominant (and you probably are, since you are reading this book), remember this fact: Google is King. We're in Google's playground. Therefore, it really only matters what Google thinks.

There are two ways to check your speed with Google:

1. Test My Site (provides a report on speed along with other aspects of your site)

2. PageSpeed Insights, which is what we will use.

You should check your website in both, but we are going to use PageSpeed Insights for this experiment.

You also need to know these two things;

1. When you check the page speed, you are just checking the speed of *that page*. This means, when you put in a link like this; www.example.com, you are just checking the speed of that page – which is the homepage. If you want to check different pages, you need to put in their exact link.
2. You need to check the speed on both mobiles and desktops. So, you will have a different value for mobile and desktop page speed.

Note: The following results are found after each plugin is installed and activated, without advanced changing of the settings. This is because this book is aimed at beginners, so I am doing this test so that the results are useful to you, someone who isn't an expert in coding and stuff!

Test 1
No 'speeding up plugins' included, website made 'as normal':

Poor
46 / 100

Poor
48 / 100

Test 2: WP Super Cache
After activating this plugin, nothing changed, so I went into the plugin settings and turned on the Caching like this;

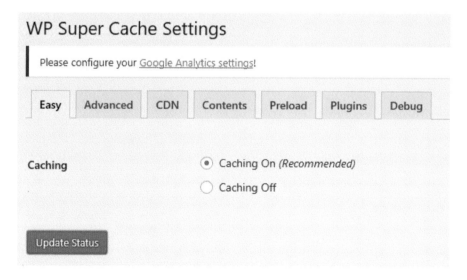

and I enabled CDN support like this;

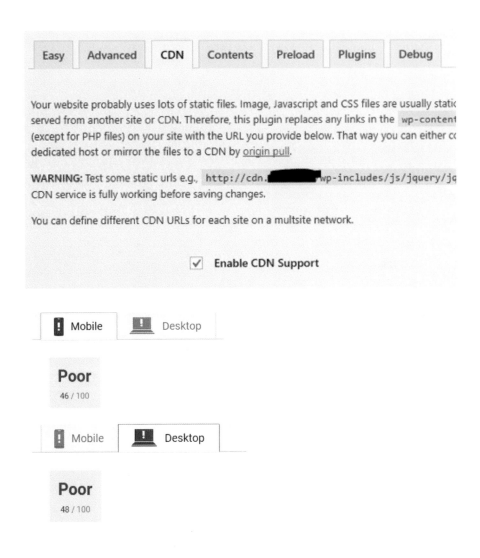

Test 3: W3 Total Cache

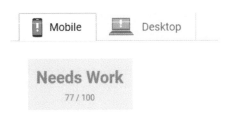

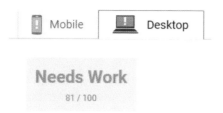

Mobile | Desktop

Needs Work
81 / 100

Test 4: WP Fastest Cache

After activating this plugin, nothing changed, so I went into the plugin settings and turned on all of these options here:

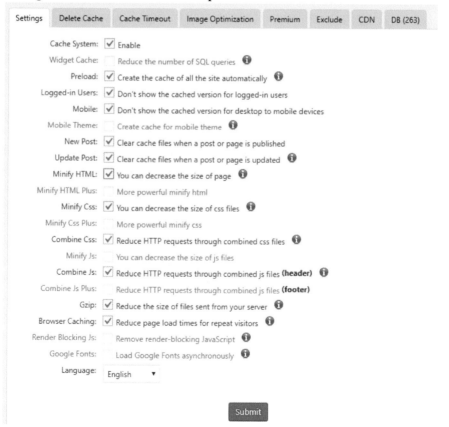

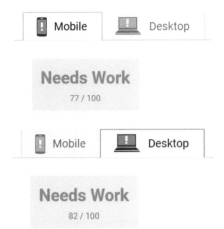

Needs Work
77 / 100

Needs Work
82 / 100

Chapter 20: Security

WordPress is no more vulnerable to hacks then other similar systems. However, its popularity makes it more *attractive* to hackers.

Updating

WordPress gets updated periodically. Most of the time, these updates are to improve security. You should keep your WordPress website updated.

e.g. here I can see when I login to my dashboard, that there is an update for WordPress;

WordPress 4.7.2 is available! Please update now.

To update, simply click in the 'Please update now' and then 'Update Now' on the next page.

N.B. Never update WordPress without doing a full backup of your site. See here.

While you don't need to update every single time you see an update available, it's a good idea to decide to update once a month.

It's also a good idea to update your plugins after you update your WordPress.

Remember that every WordPress website has its own theme. So, to change a setting on your WordPress website, may not be done in the same way on another WordPress website.

Update in this order:
1. Backup everything
2. Update WordPress
3. Update your theme
4. Update your plugins

Users

It's imperative you never give anyone your own password or login details. Always create a new account for each person who needs access to your site. Only give them access to exactly what they need. Once that person no longer needs access, delete their account.

Additionally

As you can see, this book is not going into detail into WordPress security, but it is important to at least mention it here. In previous chapters, we mentioned the plugin 'Limit Login Attempts' have been mentioned. Users were also covered: Monitor your users and who has access to your website. For an e-commerce website, or website handling sensitive data, or processing online forms, get an SSL certificate, so that your website is on https://

This also means that your website will rank better, as Google are now looking at SSL certs as a ranking factor.

Additional Resources

WordPress Support

Because you bought this book, you can ask any questions (and hopefully share any tips you find) in this Facebook group: »
www.facebook.com/groups/WordPressMasterbook

Free E-Learning Course

A new e-learning course is being developed based on this book, which will be ready sometime in mid-January. Because you purchased this book, I would like to offer you free access to this complimentary course if you are in the first 1,000 applicants. Email **info@golearndigital.com**, and mention this eBook, for unlimited free access to this course.

Images for your Site

If you put crappy images on your website, then your website will look crappy. I can't rant enough how important good imagery is for your website.

Option 1: Find Free Images using Google Search

N.B. That images you find through Google are not necessarily free to use – if you don't check, then you could be stealing. You can search for free images on Google. Instructions are here to help you: »
http://www.zonua.ie/articles/free-images-for-websites.php

Option 2: Free Stock Photography Websites:

» www.pexels.com and » www.pixabay.com are brilliant. Some other good ones are www.freepik.com and www.pxhere.com.

I keep a list of the best that I find here: » www.zonua.ie/articles/free-images.php

Option 3: Pay for Stock Photography

» www.canstockphoto.ie

» www.depositphotos.com

I keep a list of the best that I find here:

» www.zonua.ie/articles/cheapest-and-best-stock-photo-sites.php

Option 4: Ask Your Supplier

If you are selling products that you have bought from a supplier, there's a good chance that they will already have really good professional photographs of the products. Make sure you ask, and make sure you get written permission before using them, even if it's just confirmation in an email.

Option 5: Take Your Own Photographs or Pay a Professional Photographer

Assuming money and resources are no object, then the best of all of these options is to take original, brilliant, creative images. This will be best for branding and SEO.

HTML

HTML is like the building block of the web. When you make a WordPress site, WordPress automatically translates whatever you do into HTML.

Want to learn more about HTML? Check out »
www.w3schools.com/html

CSS

CSS is for styling. CSS decides that the background is a certain colour, your font is a certain type … There are certain things pre-decided in your theme. You can edit certain things yourself (e.g. the fonts) in the Appearance section. For full control, the CSS files need to be edited. Find these within *Appearance > Editor*.

N.B. Never edit these files without a full back-up. You can do serious damage here!

Want to learn CSS? » **www.w3schools.com/css**